Naked Writing: The No Frills Way to Write Your Book

By Glenys O'Connell

DEDICATION

I'd like to dedicate this book to all the students of the Naked Writing: The No Frills Way to Write Your Book creative writing course. Thank you for joining me on the publishing journey! Special thanks to authors Patricia Sands & Monika Baughman, beta readers extraordinaire!

Naked Writing: The No Frills Way to Write Your Book   Glenys O'Connell

Copyright © 2012 Glenys O'Connell

All rights reserved.

ISBN: 1477457488
ISBN-13: 978-1477457481

Inside these pages you'll learn how to:

* start writing immediately, because each chapter comes with assignments you apply to your own new or work-in-progress book.

* Identify the kind of novel you want to write, and understand the elements of a good, workable idea

* Understand story structure and how to use it to make your novel flow

* Create an outline that will get you through the dry spells of Writer's Block

* Know the important elements you must have at the start and end of each chapter

* Build characters you'll love to work with - and readers will love to read about

* Points of View - just who's telling this story, anyway?

* Develop plot points and sub-plots to add texture to your story

* Understand the two different types of character motivation - and how to use them

* Tap into the magic of dialogue, and learn when narrative and backstory can help, or hinder, your story

* Keep your story flowing to a satisfying ending with all the loose ends tied up.

BOOKS BY GLENYS O'CONNELL

Novels

Resort to Murder
Marrying Money
Winters & Somers
Judgement by Fire

Children's Books:

The Pebble People Save the Day
The Pebble People and the Lost Hero
The Pebble People Make a Garden
Rosie & the Spaceship
If Kenny Didn't Do it, Who Did?

Non-Fiction Books

Naked Writing: The No Frills Way to Write Your Book
PTSD: The Essential Guide
Depression: The Essential Guide
CultureWise Ireland

Plays

Ciara's Coming Home
(winner of awards in the All Ireland One-Act Plays Festival 2003 & Winner of the lst Prize Certificate of Excellence for Drama in the 2011 Oireachtas Gaelige Cheanada)
The Clock

CONTENTS

Introduction

Chapter One
Know Your Genre:
Chapter One Assignments

Chapter Two
Building Blocks of Story
Beginnings, Middles & Ends
Interviewing & Structure
Finding Your Story's Essence
The Novel Planner

Chapter Three
Plots & Outlines
The Novel Planner Notebook
The Very Basic Outline

Chapter Four
Hook Beginnings
Cliffhanger Endings
Writer's Block

Chapter Five
Characterization
Getting to Know Your Characters
Character Sheets

Chapter Six
Point of View (POV)
Dialogue, Narrative & Exposition
Using Dialogue

CONTENTS (cont.)

Chapter Seven
Setting the Scene
Macro Settings
Micro Settings

Chapter Eight
Seasoning with Conflict
Internal Conflict
External Conflict
Research

Chapter Nine
Motivation.
The Dreaded Sagging Middle

Chapter Ten
Editing Your Work.
Formatting.
Submitting: Finding an Agent or Publisher
Rejection Letters; Stepping Stones to Success

INTRODUCTION

As writers, we're dreamers – and I don't just mean about characters and plot lines. No, we also fantasize about our careers, about signing books while surrounded by adoring fans, of watching our titles fly up the NY Times bestseller list, of being invited to chat with Oprah, of writing non-fiction that catapults us onto the speech circuit as An Authority.

And then we daydream about what we'll do with all those millions of dollars we will earn through our writing, or how we'll parlay our growing knowledge into something that will help change people's lives.... Yes, there are probably as many dreams as there are writers when it comes to thoughts of the life we'll lead as Famous Writers Whose Books Are Bestsellers.

But here's the hard truth: these dreams have little to do with your success as a writer – unless you act on them.

To be successful you need talent, yes, and a commitment to your work. You need to mix that talent with a fair old dose of hard work to turn those dreams into your reality. The simple truth is that first and foremost, ***a writer writes***. It's that simple. The complicated bit comes in knowing what you should be writing and in planning for your success. Don't give up the dreams; just temper them with a little feet-on-the-ground common sense.

Find a way to turn them into goals. Plan your writing career as you would any other endeavor that's important to you. Dream big, for sure, but keep one eye firmly fixed on your own reality.

In fact, it seems to me that there are several secrets to being successful as a writer and getting published. Consider these:

1) **Believe in yourself and don't give up.** Writing can be disheartening at times – you sacrifice time you could be doing other things in order to write. It's hard, and sometimes it may feel that there are only rejections and it will never get any better.

2) **Write the book of your heart** - let your passion for the story shine through. Forget the idea of a 'formula' and write the book you want to read, the book that tells the story that you need to tell.

3) **Realize that a good writer is in a constant state of 'becoming' rather than 'being'** – writers should always be honing their craft, learning and growing, to constant become a better writer rather than merely a good writer

4) **Be prepared to put yourself out there -** there are many wonderful books that their creators have consigned to a box under the bed for fear of rejection, or fear of what other people might say or think. You have to believe in yourself and in the story you want to tell. What someone else thinks – be it a relative, a friend, your boss, an agent, publisher, editor, or even your creative writing teacher – counts only in so far as you can see a way to use their comments to make the book better in your own eyes.

5) **Do the work. This is the biggie** - no-one ever became a successful writer by talking about the book they're 'going to write someday'. Get the words on paper, learn your craft, learn to edit and polish, send your work out and learn from the critiques you receive from editors and agents. Then, when you're published, be prepared to promote, promote, promote….no matter how difficult you find this, or how shy you might be.

When I first began writing, back in what my kids refer to as the 'Dark Ages', by which they meant before computers and the Internet, there were few guides for writers. The ones I read were staid, intellectual treatises that made writing seem like some kind of religion only the initiated could practice.

Times changed, and with the advent of the World Wide Web, lots of information and opportunities became available to writers.

And with this deluge of information came all sorts of advice, much of it terrific. But some of it caused more confusion than clarity. You have probably come across some of these examples:

Meditate before you write

Use only pen and paper to capture your thoughts.

Light candles around your writing space – certain scents inspire creativity.

Write at dawn, when your work is blessed by the rising sun.

Write at night, when the moon inspires you to greatness.......

Yeah, right. I started my career as a journalist. Imagine the effect of announcing that I couldn't write the front page lead *until* I'd meditated, lit candles, and performed other rituals to bless my work......I'd have been quickly shown the door!

So I learned that nothing takes the place of actually getting the writing written!

And so the creative writing course known as Naked Writing: The No Frills Way to Write Your Book was born. Over the years I've worked with many students who have turned their writing dreams into published books and articles. This books is a compilation of those classes and the knowledge and insights that stem from working with enthusiastic writing students.

In this book we're going to get down to the nitty-gritty of writing. We're going to roll up our sleeves and work hard. No candles, no chants, no meditating (unless you feel the need!) Just dreaming and planning and writing. All the way to The End.

Are you ready to start? Of course you are!

But Before We Begin, a Little Writerly Wisdom:

Whatever your writing ambitions, you need a plan. Consider these points:

1) **A dream is not a goal** – recognize the difference between your writerly dreams, and what would really satisfy you. Ask yourself why you write – would you be surprised to find that the answer isn't necessarily 'to get rich' or 'to be famous?

2) **It's not just time – you need a plan** - despite what you may have been told about writing every day, there are lots of successful writers who hold down full time jobs and squeeze in their writing at weekends. Their secret? They plan their work and work the plan.

3) **A dose of reality** – if you've considered #1 above, you know where your 'success satisfaction' lies. Now decide what sort of writing will take you there.

4) **Writing is hard, lonely work** - why are you doing this to yourself? What can you do to ensure your precious writing time is your own without becoming a hermit? Consider setting up a 'support network' of other writers (the Internet is a great resource for this!) There are lists where writers share triumphs and setbacks and encourage each other – but who understand that the writing always comes first...

5) **Whittle away the fat** - identify your writing goals. Having a road map for your writing career will help prevent you from going off at tangents that steal time, energy & creativity and prevent you from reaching your writerly destination.

6) **Knowing what you want to achieve** - and drawing up a plan gives you an overview. This overview allows you to list the actions you need to take. These can be broken down further into 'Baby Steps' which let you utilize even small segments of spare time to take your ambitions a little further ahead.

7) **Setting up your goal calendar** which outlines the tiny steps forward and shows where the giant leaps and bounds can happen.
8) **Be open minded** - so many different types of writing work – novels, articles, copywriting, teaching, editing, speechwriting, speaking….oh my! Keeping an open mind about opportunities and where they might lead you will help you pick the best writing and promotional opportunities for your career.
9) **Career planning 101** - now that you know where you're going don't forget to pencil in some time to evaluate each stage to make sure you're on track, or if you need to adjust your plans or change direction. Stuff happens!
10) **Learn to cope with distractions** - be decisive in handling everyday crises and don't let the little things become big time stealers. You need to keep all those plates spinning at once – family, friends, day job, health, etc. – and still write. Believe me, cars and appliances break down, kids need you to volunteer at school, relatives need care, big projects will come up at work, and friends need a shoulder to cry on. All these things will continue to happen whether you're writing or not. You will be calmer and more cheerful about dealing with them if you've been able to do your writing quota! There are many resources with tips for writing & coping with living – search the Internet for your own favorites.

Ready? Flex your typing fingers, and away we go!

CHAPTER ONE:

This first chapter looks at markets, audiences and publishers for the sort of book you want to write, and at what kind of genre/category your book fits into. It might seem odd to think of marketing before you've written your book, but students of my writing course tell me that this exercise helps to focus you on your idea and to clarify what you want to do.

Don't take this as meaning that you should try to write a book that fits with other books on the market. What it really means is to get to know what is already out there, who's buying what. This will give you an advantage when choosing the theme and voice of your book and determining freshness of your plot and story, among other things.

It's also the perfect excuse to go browse around the bookstores - and what writer can refuse that? If you can't get into an actual store, go online and visit Amazon, Barnes and Noble, Indigo/Chapters, etc. and look at the categories like mystery, romantic suspense, romance, thrillers, historical, women's literature, etc. Whatever areas you are interested in. See what area the authors you like are filed in - as writers, we often write the kind of book we like to read!

KNOW YOUR GENRE

Go into any large bookstore and you'll be dazzled by the wide array of books, the subjects and the variety, all awaiting your eager purchase. But you're moving beyond being a mere bookstore browser - you're a writer and one day soon you're planning to see your own book decorating those shelves. But what kind of book are you writing?

You can see from the shelves there that there are many different kinds. Are you writing mainstream? These are books with a more general appeal, as opposed to say, category romance. Mysteries, crime, literary, biography, docu-drama, science fiction, futuristic, military, gothic, horror, suspense, humour, fantasy, erotica…..

There's even a section called Women's Literature. It may strike you as wrong that women's literature should be separated out from Literature as if it's somehow inferior, which of course it isn't But when you think about it, there are subjects dealt with in this genre that appeal specifically to women. Often they look at relationships, motherhood, sexuality, and survival in a patriarchal society. And the other bonus is that, if you're writing a thoughtful literary novel unveiling some of the issues that intrigue or disturb you, you may well have an edge in getting published in this category.

Even most of the genres have sub-genres: detective novels, for example, have 'cosies', a sort of modern day English country house mystery, and 'hard-boiled' which is the tough private-eye kind of story as made popular by Dashiel Hammett. Then there are detective mysteries, which can be 'hard-boiled' or 'amateur'; police procedurals, private eye novels, or law-and-order police types.

There are the category romances, which are a specialist genre in their own right. If I were to say to you that I was reading a Harlequin Romance, you'd probably immediately have a picture in your mind of a fairly sexy cover, and an idea of a book in which the entire story usually revolves around the growing love relationship between a hero and heroine (I say usually - there are many changes coming down the pipeline, and some companies are publishing books for gay and lesbian relationships, etc. Not Harlequin, Mills & Boon yet, though).

In these stories, everything comes secondary to the love relationship. However, they are category romances because they can be split into categories: you have sweet, sexy, hot, tender, and then you've got medical, suspense, paranormal....all crowding together under the same general heading of category romance.

Now, the reason for knowing what genre your about-to-be-written book falls into is not so that you can put out a cookie-cutter version of the latest best seller in that genre. The idea is to find out what's already out there and who publishes it.

Also, consider the kind of books you enjoy reading. Writers often start out by writing the sort of book they would like to read. List your favourite authors. It's important for writers to read and keep up with current trends. Keep the receipts because in most jurisdictions you can claim books, magazines, etc., as a business expense for your writing. Even if you're making no money from your writing yet, most tax jurisdictions give you a couple of years to get started, allowing you to claim tax relief on your expenses, including your computer, travel, paper, workshops, etc.

Sometimes they may ask to see some evidence that you are writing seriously and attempting to earn an income, so make sure you also keep copies of the letters you will send out to publishers, and the replies you get - even the rejections count for something in the taxman's eyes! Check with your local tax office for further details of what you can claim.

Chapter One Assignments:

Writing Exercise One: Consider one or more of your favourite books, and write a few sentences about what aspects appeal to you, specific reasons you liked the book: was it story, plot points, characters, setting, genre....?

Writing Exercise Two: Going to the bookstore and browsing the books was no hardship, right? But wait - there's more:

Take a note of the titles in the same general category or genre as the one you plan to write. List their publishers, and if you can, copy down a couple of blurbs from the back or inside cover. You know, the parts that offer a (usually) enticing couple of paragraphs about the story, designed to lure you into buying. And by all means, buy a book, or two or three.

Your next step is to look up the publishers on your list from the bookshop. Use the Writers' Market or Writers' And Artists Yearbook if you have one - it's invaluable for writers. You don't need to buy a new one every year, but do remember that publishing personnel can move around a lot between companies, so it's usually a good idea to phone or check their Internet listing when you're ready to submit to ensure the editor in the section you're targeting is still there. Or get the new editor's name, no matter how recent your Writer's Market is. There is also an online version.

You can also do online searches for the publishers' websites. Look for 'submissions' (it's sometimes hidden away under the 'contact us' or 'about us' buttons) You will find that many publishers don't accept submissions from unagented writers, which can be a bit of a catch 22 situation as it can be hard to get an agent interested until you're published.

Look through the publishers' sites; look at what they're publishing now that's similar to the sort of book you're planning to write. If you can get guidelines for submissions, and if they tell you what they're looking for, you're streets ahead. Are they looking for stories with lots of action? What level of sexual content predominates? Do they have a lot of humour, or are there mostly dark, edgy titles?

Basically, familiarise yourself with the publishers' requirements, and keep a list and notes - sometime soon you're going to be targeting these publishers. While you are not going to be writing a book deliberately pushed into a specific shape to fit a publisher, you are going to keep one eye on the market as you write. This way you can enhance any aspects of your own work you perceive that publishers want. Keep these notes - they'll help you when you start sending work off.

Don't ignore electronic publishers, either. The pundits are telling us that this is the way of the future and, in my humble opinion; electronic publishing is an exciting field that holds lots of potential for writers. Many epublishers put out a print version of their books. You can surf the internet and find epublishers quite easily. Check out their guidelines in the same way you did the bookstore publishers, but don't be fooled into thinking that it's easier to get published as an ebook author. The last statistics I saw show that the ratio of manuscripts received to books published is pretty much the same for both print and ebook publishers.

Don't worry if you're thinking this is all about research, and you want to get on with the writing. Marketing, and understanding the market, is an important part of writing. This will become evident as we go along.

In Chapter Two, we're going to start a worksheet, and look at story structure. Have fun in the bookstores!

CHAPTER TWO

Now is the time to create a routine to get you into the habit of doing some work on your writing and on your writing objectives on a regular basis. It may not be every day, but try to set up a routine for writing so that when you sit down at your computer or notebook at a designated time, your brain registers that **now** is the time to write.

Consider your routines – when can you make time to write? When do you feel most inspired? Pencil in some times in your daybook, to remind yourself that this is time set aside for your writing career.

After the trip to the bookstore in Chapter One - which wasn't exactly a hardship, was it? - we're rolling up our sleeves and getting down to growing your novel idea into a book.

Chapters Two and Three have a lot of material in them, and the Assignments need some thought, so take your time with them so that you have this part of your story 'foundation' built solidly.

What we are doing in this chapter is to boil your story down to its essence, then write that 'kernel' down, along with setting up a working title and noting the likely genre. Distilling your story into a few sentences is surprisingly beneficial.

For one thing, it keeps you in touch with the basic storyline, especially if you pin it up near your favourite writing spot or workstation. A working title makes the book more real – it's no longer the work-in-progress, or the book, but in your head you're seeing a real book with a title. You'll be surprised at the difference that can make in the way you look at it – it's no longer anonymous, but a real book!

Secondly, writing a 'logline' or few sentences will show how strong the story idea is. A 'blurb' that can grab the reader is a strong idea, while one that leaves you wondering in a 'yes, but...' fashion needs a little extra plot work.

We'll also be working on the very important aspect of beginnings, middles and ends - the secret ingredients to keeping your story flowing and your reader turning the pages.

THE BUILDING BLOCKS OF STORY:

Every story should have a beginning, a middle, and an end in order to be complete. You learned that in school, right?

Of course, but like everything else in writing, when you come to write the story it's not quite so simple as it sounds to have that Beginning, Middle and End.

BEGINNINGS: Where should your story begin? New writers often make the mistake of starting long before the real story begins in an attempt to get their reader orientated. But think about this for a moment. If you were to tell someone about your day, how would you start? Would you begin by describing how you woke up, got up, ate, dressed and went about your daily work, right down to the details of dental flossing and crisping the bacon just the way you like it?

Of course not - you'd start at, or just before, a point where something interesting, something unusual, happens. The reader can assume that your protagonist (main character) got out of bed that morning and got his or her day going something like the way the rest of us do - except, of course, unless the unusual event starts as he wakes up, like the bedroom ceiling collapsing on him....

So, consider where your story actually starts. Let's make up an example. Suppose your hero was orphaned when his parents died in a car wreck when he was only five. He had a difficult time being raised in foster homes, or maybe he had a good life with loving adoptive parents. But now he's 31 and is just opening his mail on a sunny Tuesday morning. There is a letter from someone purporting to be an old friend of his long-dead father, claiming that Dad never died in a car smash but has been living in Las Vegas under an assumed name all these years.

Where does the story start? ***With the opening of the letter; this is the beginning of the hero's quest to find out the truth.*** The details of his childhood are all interesting backstory - in fact, you could perhaps have a prologue where the car accident takes place, work in something a little fishy, and show how he came to believe he was orphaned. Details of his life after that - abusive or loving home - can be worked into the story in little pieces as we go along, and they will add colour and richness to his character.

Each beginning is special - you choose what we call a 'hook' or particularly exciting statement to open with. We'll be discussing this later.

MIDDLES: The middle is the rock on which many a good novel founders. This is where you run out of steam, unless you've done some good planning beforehand. I always suggest that writers be careful with the amount of planning they do. If you do too much outlining it can feel as if you've already written the story and you lose the excitement which is so important in carrying you through to the end.

We'll be talking about outlines and planning later. But the main thing that gets you through the middle is applying the beginning, middle and end structure to *every chapter*. Each chapter is a scene, or perhaps more than one scene depending on length and each scene has a beginning, a middle, and an end in action. Therefore, instead of 250 - 350 pages with one beginning, one middle and one end, you are actually going to write your novel with possibly ten or 20 beginnings, middles and ends. We will discuss this more thoroughly; I just want you to be aware of this now.

ENDS: Often when the story idea strikes, you'll also have some idea how it ends, or how you want it to end - sometimes when you're writing, what you want and what actually happens can be different. However, it works much better if you know what you want the ending to be. This way you can shape your story so that it moves organically towards that ending. Endings should always be satisfying, and if you have a little surprise in there, all the better. But you must tie up all the loose ends and clues and hints you've scattered throughout the previous 200 or so pages.

Endings need to be logical - think of the old westerns, when the wagons were circled and it looked as though the Indians would win the day, when suddenly the US Cavalry arrived over the hills in the nick of time. As a child I always used to wonder how the cavalry knew the wagon train needed their help - they didn't have cell phones then, so just how did they know to show up?

This loose end bothered me enormously - don't let loose ends like this bother your readers... Make sure you tidy everything up, so that each hint you dropped is shown to have a satisfactory place within your story by the end. If you are enthusiastic and lay too many hints, clues and red herrings, or you have a sub plot that doesn't actually develop because you decided not to follow through with it, and then eliminate it from your story. Be ruthless.

Stephen King uses the phrase 'Kill Your Darlings' for this! You want your reader to feel satisfied when reaching the end of your book, and think: ***Well, the ending was a bit of a surprise, but gee, I can see now it was really the only way this story could end!***

INTERVIEWING AND STRUCTURE

In any story, there is a structure – and this is the same for fiction and non-fiction, although the jargon may vary.

The bits inside the story have the same format, too, with the ones in fiction roughly correlating to those in non-fiction:

> Characters = Who?
> Storyline = What?
> Motivation = Why?
> Timeline = When?
> Setting = Where?

When you interview someone for a story, whether it's a real person or a character in your story, the *who* is vitally important. **Who** is more than the person's name. It's their occupation, or the part they play in the story.

What is what's happening right now – i.e., a creative writing class.

Why is why is it happening, **why** is the person doing what they are doing?

When – is when the event is occurring? It could be the time of the person's life, a thousand years into the future, an earlier century, or any other computation of time.

Where – is the setting of the story. A writing group meeting right now, or a raging battle between empires in the 24th century in a galaxy far away. A Victorian drawing room, a city you've never visited, or a loofah barbecue on Planet Mars. Whatever your writing tastes lean towards…..

These questions are just as important as for non-fiction. They add texture and realism to your work.

Consider now that you are building a story 'house'. Your basement is the story idea, your plot is the foundation, and your outline is the floor. The chapters with their beginnings and endings are your walls, and the characters who draw all this together and speak the lines are your roof. You then furnish this building with plumply upholstered motives and lovingly polished events, and you accent with colourful conflicts. Wouldn't you just love to live there?

FINDING YOUR STORY'S ESSENCE

After your foray into the bookstores and contemplation of beginnings, middles and ends, we're going to start getting down to some real writing.

First of all, write down your novel idea. How long is your description? A few pages? A page? Three paragraphs? A couple of sentences?

If your answer was the last option, a couple of sentences, then you're in luck. That's exactly what I want you to do - boil your entire story idea down into two or three crisp, bright sentences. This usually sets students off into groans and moans, but later when they realise what a valuable exercise it is, they're delighted.

Why should you express your idea in so few words? Several reasons:

1) You want to know how strong your idea is. Will it last to The End?

If you are able to write it down in two or three sentences, and it still makes sense and sparkles brightly, then you can be fairly sure you've a workable idea. If not, it might be that you need to set it aside until other parts of the puzzle pop into your head.

I always keep an 'ideas file' on my computer. I used to just scribble down notes, but in the end I had several purses crammed with bits of paper, receipts, and paper napkins, all with unintelligible scribbles that once were great ideas. I still scribble down ideas when they come to me - but as soon as I can, I type them into my computer file. Funnily enough, by the time I do this I have a lot more detail for the idea.

Antidote for a Weak Idea: Set it aside in your Ideas File, and read it every now and again - strengthening additions will occur to you. Look at your file to see if any other ideas can be merged to form a stronger whole. Ideas do not arrive in our heads fully formed, sometimes they come in bits and pieces and the smart writer is alert enough to capture them as they arrive.

2) Now you have this one paragraph mini outline. It keeps you focused on your story. Write it out on sticky notes and apply to your computer monitor, your diary - even the bathroom mirror if you dare!

3) This short form is your pitch to an editor or agent. In screenwriting, it's called a 'logline' and is used to capture the attention of producers and directors. In our case, we're going to nurture this simple paragraph, use it at the beginning of query letters and as the basis for the synopsis which is our selling tool when the book is finished and ready to do the rounds of publishers and agents.

See how useful this logline is? So how do you do it?

Take the most important part of your idea, add the names of the two main characters, and describe the problem they must overcome. Here are some examples from well-known books:

Consider these:

A young couple fall in love and vow to remain together despite the opposition of their families and an edict from the ruling prince, but a misunderstanding brings about tragic consequences - **Romeo and Juliet**

A rebel leader goes up against the might of Rome, is betrayed by his own people, and is martyred. But his teachings of love and peace live on and are still celebrated 2000 years later – **The New Testament**

A man and woman struggle against powerful opposition to solve the riddle of an ancient code and find a precious artefact. They learn the truth about it, and in doing so they learn the truth about themselves and fall in love. But when they find the artefact and realise the dangers it could pose, they decide to keep its secret safe forever - **The Da Vinci Code**

A man whose family has worked a piece of land for generations believes it should be his, and is willing to kill to hold onto it. But his stubbornness results in the death of his only surviving son and he is left to question the true value of the land he so coveted - **The Field**.

Your logline will probably be a bit longer than these, because you want to get in names of the main characters, the problem they face, etc. Here are two examples from books I'm working on right now:

A Romantic Suspense:

Psychologist and wannabe playwright Gracie Pelham is thrilled when the local theatre group puts on one of her plays…until someone adds a real dead body to the props. Gracie finds herself playing the role of investigator while balancing her list of crazy clients and, just when she thinks life can't get any worse, in comes her gorgeous soon-to-be-ex-husband as the police detective in charge of the case. They'd been fighting like cat and dog before the breakup, but working together resurrects feelings they can't ignore. And finally they can agree on something: Neither of them wants to see Gracie cast as the next victim….but can they unmask the killer before the final curtain call?

A Young Adult:

Canadian teen Jenna Graham isn't too impressed when her mother inherits an Irish aristocratic title; she's even less thrilled when she's dragged along to claim the inheritance and the family seat turns out to be a decaying mansion with hostile neighbors and a passel of strangely familiar ghosts. Meeting

Liam Dunbar helps cheer her up – but their budding romance is the catalyst that re-ignites the estate's bloody history. Jenna is haunted by terrifying dreams of past lives in which lovers have been torn apart, while her mother begins to act even more strangely, and she finds herself locked in a battle to undo her ancestors' sins and save Liam from a violent death as history repeats itself …..

See what's there? The two main characters, the problem, a little background, and a suggestion as to what must be done for the ending. Now for the Writing Assignments ………….

Chapter Two Writing Assignments.

Writing Exercise 2:1 Fill in the work planner (below) with the working title for your novel - this can change, of course, it's just that you become so much more committed to the project when you've named it! Then fill in the genre or type of book it is, and last of all, write in your name after By: Imagine how this will look on the cover of your manuscript, or better yet, imagine it on the full colour cover of your published book! Give yourself a few moments to savour the feeling!

Writing Exercise 2:2 Write a short blurb or 'logline' that describes your story. Fill in this section of the work planner (below). Read through the Novel Work Planner and answer as many of the questions as you can. It works best if you can photocopy it and keep it at your writing desk – fill in the details as they come to you while you're writing. Right now, though, make sure you fill in the title, genre, and author and blurb at the very least! As you work through the chapters, come back and fill in more of the Novel Work Planner. This part has been put on separate pages to make photocopying or scanning easier:

THE NOVEL WORK PLANNER

Working Title: _____

A _____ **Novel**
By _____

Blurb (logline):

Main Characters:
1)

2)

3)

4)

Hook:

Setting/Time:

Problem #1

Consequences:

Problem #2

Consequences:

Problem #3

Consequences:

Solution & Victory:

Dark Moment:

Final Victory & Ending:

CHAPTER THREE

Plots & outlines are fairly well entwined, and form the core of one of the many writing details that writers argue about. Most of us agree that you need to have a plot to have a good book – and that goes for non-fiction as well, because the plot is the core, the book's raison d'étre, if you will. The plot is the vehicle for your message, your theme – it carries what you are saying to your reader.

Outlines, however, are even more hotly debated. Some writers claim they can't live without them, and some claim to write up to 90 pages of outline details. Others swear they are a waste of time and interfere with the 'free flow' of the story.

Personally, I believe there is a happy middle ground here. A brief outline, or even a slightly more detailed one, helps to keep you on track with the story without wandering off on all those other enticing little highways and byways that appear as you write. The latter can lead you into an entirely new story – or into getting lost entirely. On the other hand, keeping your outline brief allows space for you to see opportunities for further angles or sub-plots, and room to include them, without losing the path you want your story to take.

It's all individual taste, so I suggest that you try both methods mentioned here, as well as any other possibilities that occur to you, and also see if writing by the seat of your pants (pantsering!) works for you. It may be a question of trial and error – for some books you may find the story just leaps from your head onto the page with no need for an outline, while others cry out for a structured way of writing. Experiment and find out what works best for you.

Most of all enjoy the writing journey!

In this chapter we look at the structure of stories and the different types of plots and the importance of having a brief outline. Also, how to put together the outline in either brief or the more elaborate novel planner notebook method. We also take a look at the Hero's Journey for story structure.

PLOTS AND OUTLINES

There are basically two kinds of stories – plot driven and character driven.

Plot driven stories depend strongly on the events – war stories, for example – rather than on the characters. You can have a person or group of people placed in a specific situation and they are reacting all the time to the events – escaping capture, surviving the prison camp, or whatever.

We do not look at their motives – the events themselves provide motivation. We also don't generally look at the way the events cause the characters to change. Instead, we follow them as they act and react physically to the things that happen to them.

Character driven stories, on the other hand, are all about the characters' reactions, motivations, and the way they change through the experience of the events they have to cope with. Most stories today rely on this kind of plot.

For example, let's invent a character named Bill. Bill's beloved grandmother, with whom he lived, had a heart attack when she was forcibly evicted from her home years ago. At that time Bill, a boy of 12, swore he'd never be poor or homeless again. He vowed to ruthlessly follow a career that would make him wealthy and powerful. Bill works for a development company and is doing very well, thank you.

The story starts when Bill has an opportunity to acquire a valuable piece of real estate, the development of which will make him rich. But the existing tenants must be evicted.

One of the tenants, an old lady, comes to see him with her grandson to plead for his intervention to save her home. It's a situation which mirrors Bill's childhood experience. What is he going to do? Will he sneer and follow his dreams of ruthless wealth? Or will he find the ice melting around his heart as he is thrown back to his own childhood, and decide to change his behaviour and become a nicer, gentler person by championing these helpless tenants? And what will happen to him within the organization he works for, if he does that?

This goes to character, motivation, consequences, and change. Always ask yourself what your character has to gain and lose through their actions, what motivates them, and why. Bill is at a crossroads. He has been so determined that his past experiences would never occur again that he has now put himself in the position of treating other vulnerable people the way he was treated. What path will he choose?

Outlines: Your story outline must start at the breathless moment when your main character is, or is about to be, dropped into a situation which is very problematic for him/her. For example, we could have started the story when Bill was a child about to lose his home. This might make a prologue, but the real story begins when Bill is faced with the decision about whether he will remain true to his vow of getting rich, in which case he becomes the kind of person he hated as a child, or whether he will change direction and learn from the lessons of his childhood to become a better person.

Another name for this is the Hero's Journey. Joseph Campbell analysed myths and came up with a sequence that is common to all stories – the Hero's Journey. Chris Vogler turned this into the writer's journey, creating a rough list of the events you need to have in your story.

This starts out with the hero being given a problem, one he must solve, and one which shakes him out of his snug world. He may balk, try to refuse the assignment, and then something else happens which forces him to choose. As a result of that choice, he faces a journey through the consequences until he wins through – and is changed forever.

In this way the plot becomes a series of highly charged events which work on the protagonist and create change. Writer Alicia Rastley says: '....the primary purpose of a plot is to give the protagonist (your main character) a reason to change in the direction he or she needs to change. It is a vehicle for the character's journey to growth.'

Use this concept to create an outline for your story. Consider the best beginning - it might not be at the very moment the crisis event that precipitates the story occurs, but it should be close to that moment. Or you can have a brief prologue, but it must be relevant and not give away too much of the plot.

Outlines come in several forms. One is a simple a point-by-point list of the main plot events – I call this the Very Brief Outline (see the brief outline below). The idea is to note down the plot points quickly in short form, and work from there. This is a very good way of doing it, as you have guideposts but you don't have so much detail that you feel 'stuck'. This makes it easier to be creative and expand or change the story direction.

Another route is the Novel Planner Notebook - see novel planner notebook item below. I've found this one very good for writing quickly when you are sure of the direction you intend to take. In my experience, it is best for shorter books or for children's midgrade or young adult novels. Using this method, you keep close track of your writing, filling in a calendar of pages written, and you keep the important details of all your characters as they grow, all in one place. This way you can avoid someone having green eyes and black hair in chapter two and becoming a blue-eyed blond in chapter eight!

The notebook provides a place to keep a chronology of events as they occur, which can be very useful in avoiding embarrassing things like one of the characters having a 13 month pregnancy…..yes, these things have occurred in novels, and yes, readers have written in to tell the embarrassed writer of the mistake!

The notebook has plastic pockets into which you insert a brief outline for each chapter, and when that chapter is finished, you put a print out of it in the same pocket, so the notebook grows fat and satisfying. There's also space for you to keep notes of any research you've done, so this is a very comprehensive way of outlining and writing. It does help you write quickly and keep track of all the details. The only drawback is that you need to have a pretty thorough knowledge of what is going to happen all the way through the book.

Some people use a synopsis of the book as their outline, which of course doubles as a synopsis to be sent out to agents and editors with your submission package. This can work well, but it is very sketchy and you would need to be confident using it. Another drawback is that it doesn't really give you guideposts, so you may easily wander off track or find your story turns out very differently from your initial idea. Which can be a good thing or a bad thing, depending on the end result!

One thing to be careful about with outlines is that part of the joy of writing is creating and telling a story. If you put too much detail into the outline - and I've heard of people writing a 90 page outline for a 280 page book - then you may unconsciously feel that you've already told the story and find yourself bored and losing interest quickly when you set about writing it.

So, now try writing your own outline. Experiment with styles a little, enjoy the process of thinking out the plot, use the Hero's Journey as a rough guide to the flow of the story and the pivotal moments, and remember that you want to show that the events have brought about some change in your characters over the space of the story.

It may well be that you are a 'pantser' - a writer who writes by 'the seat of your pants' or spontaneously without an outline. This method works well for some people and you'll very quickly know if you are one of them. But doing an outline is a great exercise, so do give it a try. It also makes for faster writing. You may find that you adapt the outline idea to suit your own style as you gain more experience.

Don't sweat this; writing is to be enjoyed. Keep your outline functional, fairly brief so that you have room to be creative in the actual writing, and remember, outlines aren't carved in stone. Sometimes, those pesky characters don't want to act out the story you outlined it, and you need to have the space to change direction.

THE NOVEL PLANNER NOTEBOOK

The novel planner notebook acts as a 'roadmap' for your story – and it can work, in one form or another, for anything you are writing. You might not want to get this complex for short articles or poetry, but the framework of outline and detail logging is useful for these, too. The notebook is a great tool for short stories, novels, novellas, children's books, non-fiction books, family histories, etc.

I must give author Phyllis Whitney (Guide to Fiction Writing, 1982, The Writer Inc. Publishers) credit for the initial idea for this system. Until I discovered it, I was a 'seat of the pants' writer – churning out the words and pages but with no clear idea where I was going, and often getting stuck, mired in my own thoughts and ideas, along the way.

The novel planner notebook provides pointers for each chapter as well as a basic outline of the story, and prompts you as to research you'll need to get started. A word of warning, though – for some writers, compiling the novel notebook can become an adventure in itself and they make the whole thing so detailed they pretty well have no story left to write. Don't try to have every base covered when you put this book together, or you'll lose the excitement of telling the story when you actually sit down to write. The novel notebook IS NOT a substitute for the actual novel, no matter how hard you've worked on it!

Basically, the notebook involves organising your thoughts, ideas, characters, odd ideas and scenes, chronology, and research materials into one easy to access spot. No more searching through your handbag or coat pocket for that old paper napkin or receipt that you scribbled a scene on. Once upon a time, the only time my desk got tidied was when I was forced to methodically sift through the layers of accumulated paperwork to find a character description or vital piece of research that I knew I'd just 'popped down' there - somewhere.

So, on to the Novel Planner Notebook:

* You'll need a loose leaf binder, one inch for most projects, larger for a full length novel or non-fiction book with a lot of chapters and research.

*A couple of pads of lined paper, the ones that come with holes ready punched in the sides to fit the binder.

* Plastic pockets to hold loose sheets.

* Coloured divider pages with tabs. The only reason I suggest coloured ones is that they are easy to identify and they look prettier!

The first section is **Calendar**. Put a couple of sheets of blank lined paper here, write Calendar on the top. Then near the top, on one side write: **Plotting Begun** – then the date. Below that comes **Plotting Finished** – and the date. Do the same for **Research, characterization, outlining,** etc., putting a start and finishing date as you go along. This way, when you feel you've been working on this book forever, you can glance back and see the progress you've made – *my, did I really do this much since Christmas?????*

On the next page, still under the calendar heading, put the proposed word length of your book, divide it by 250 for pages, and then divide it by the number of chapters you expect to work with. This gives you the rough page count for your chapters, i.e., a 75,000-word novel is 300 pages, divided by 20 chapters is 15 pages per chapter.

You can allocate a certain number of pages per writing session, if you're really organised and able to set a specific time aside. If you know you can write 5 pages an hour and you regularly have one hour per writing session, then you'll have a chapter in three days.

Multiply that by 10 chapters, and writing every day that's a rough draft in a month! But don't get too excited – some days the words won't flow, some days you have to break off to do research, and some days, well, some scenes are just too complex, emotional, or otherwise difficult and you may only get one page done. Nice thought, though! And quite a number of category novelists write four, five, or six books a year, so it is do-able.

List **Chapter One, Chapter Two**, etc., in the left hand column. Underneath each chapter number, write **planned page number – 15.** Write **date started, page # started** the chapter on, **date finished, actual pages** of chapter, **page # chapter ends**. Six columns. This lets you know your progress, how you are doing with your page/word target, and keeps track of the chapter pages to make it easy to look up an event you know happened in chapter six, because you've got the page numbers right there. No searching through the manuscript.

Some people find it's a good incentive to also add, again under calendar, a two-column list with **'date'** and **'pages written'**. This lets you keep track of how hard (or not!) you are working. If you don't have pages for a specific date, but you were researching, rewriting, or editing, then put that down. This gives you a sense of accomplishment and encouragement.

Alternatively, a lot of blank days tells you that you really should be getting BIC HOK TAM – writer-ese for Butt In Chair, Hands On Key Board, Typing Away Madly!

I use an Excel spread sheet to keep track of pages, and another one to keep track of writing income on a week-to-week basis.

The next section is **Chronology**. This is a double section and you can add an extra divider. Section one is a quick sketch of the events you want to happen in each chapter. It allows you to see where you have gaps in the action, gauge your pacing, and check that events are taking part in the proper order.

The second part is an actual chronology of events. It says when your story takes place, over what period of time, and allows you to work out time-scales that make it all realistic. This avoids gaffes like the famous 13 month pregnancy, for example.

Next, a few blank sheets in the section called **Theme & Situation**. As your story unfolds you will begin to sense a theme – the message your story has for your readers. Once you know this, you will be able to 'plant' little clues and hints as the story goes along, and keep everyone's actions and words in keeping with the message you're sending. All this, without hitting your reader over the head with your theme!

Now we get to **Plotting**. Here you take the basic idea of your story and keep on adding all those odd and disjointed bits that arrive in your head out of sequence and in awkward moments but which, when polished and laid out in the right spot, will form your book. We aren't worried about the right spot yet, we just want to get them written down.

The next section is **Characters**. A page for each main character. Secondary characters can share a page with others, so long as you don't mix them up – we don't want Fred to have long blonde hair and a fondness for stiletto heels, unless you are actually writing *that* kind of book.

Write down all the details that pop into your head about your characters. Physical details, obviously, but also their little idiosyncrasies and the funny things they've been whispering in your ear ever since you first breathed life into them, or since they adopted you as their chronicler. I'm never sure, myself, which it is. Add details about their past lives, even though you might never refer to this in your book, and their relationship to other characters.

We're getting to the end now. The next section is **Research**, with sub-sections of **To Look Up, Bibliography** and then headings for each topic you have researched, preferably with URL's or other references. Keep a record of page numbers for any item you're querying. In this way you keep a running list of items you need to check – this stops you hitting a brick wall and having to stop writing when you don't know something.

You make a note and carry on with your writing, knowing you won't forget to research that detail. You keep a bibliography that lists all your sources, in case you need to go back again. And you write or print out all the research that you think you may need, as you come across it, and put it in individual plastic pockets in this section, filed by subject.

We're getting into the nitty-gritty. The next section is **Outline**. Here you start to pull together all the odds and ends that appeared under **Plotting**, bearing in mind everything from **Chronology**, and roughly following your chapter outlines. And Voila! You have a map of your story.

Now it gets exciting. The next section is **Chapters – Writing**. Here you are going to type out, on individual sheets of paper, the short rough outline for each chapter. These go into the binder, and behind each one goes a plastic pocket. Into that plastic pocket goes a hard copy of the chapter belonging to each chapter outline. It feels so good as this part of the binder gets fatter and fatter!

So, now you're working on your book. You're filling up those plastic pockets as you round out each chapter outline, and you've got your novel outline, character guides, chronology, situation, and theme and plotting sections to help if you get stuck. You'll almost certainly be adding to the character, plotting, chronology and outline pages as you go along and the book grows and flowers.

And that's it for the Novel Planner Notebook. As you work you may come up with your own way of putting together this novel roadmap, dropping some of the sections I recommend and adding others of your own. You'll find, too, that the make-up of the planner may vary depending on what you are actually writing. But without a doubt, the notebook makes you think about what you are doing, think out your book in detail, and iron out some of those awful glitches and roadblocks so that your writing journey is smoother, faster and a whole lot more fun!

Check your word processing program for ways of making the notebook easier to create directly on your computer if you prefer this to a hard copy binder. For example, MS Office has the very useful OneNote function that lets you build a Novel Planner Notebook right on your computer, making it easy to refer to as you write.

VERY BASIC OUTLINE:

This is a quickie outline I use as an example in classes of a point-by-point brief outline:

1. Bob Mitchell has wanted to be a priest since he was an altar boy. He feels a deep devotion to the tenets of his religion, but he is also ambitious. He believes he can do more for his Church and his people by getting into the upper echelons rather than serving in a poor ministry.
2. To do this he actively sought the mentorship of a man he greatly admired, Bishop Nonesuch. The Bishop sees the potential of this young man and has offered him both friendship and advice in pursuing his career in the church.
3. Bob is now in the running for a promotion, one which will allow him to influence decisions at a high level. Excited and validated by the prospect, he celebrates with the Bishop.

4. A young boy approaches Bob and drops the bombshell – Bishop Nonesuch is a member of a paedophilia ring. This is Bob's challenge: he must choose between rejecting the boy's story so as to continue with his ambitions and his friendship with the Bishop, believing that once he is in a more powerful position he can solve such problems. Or he can choose to act for the boy, possibly risking losing everything he has worked for.
5. Bob chooses to turn a blind eye and work seek the promotion. His conscience forces him to tentatively approach the Bishop and mention his meeting with the boy in the vaguest of terms. The Bishop reassures him that he has done the right thing and he respects Bob for this; he assures him that the boy is mentally disturbed and there is no truth to the story. However, he promises to look into the matter and see that the boy receives the treatment he needs. He also assures Bob that the promotion he seeks is his as a faithful colleague.
6. The boy is found dead, an apparent suicide. Bob feels as though he failed the child by not doing more.
7. Bob receives a letter that the boy wrote before he died, saying that he has been threatened and that his story was the truth - if anything happened to him it would not be suicide because he has faith in the Church's teachings. This is confirmed when Bob is approached by the boy's distraught sister.
8. Bob agonizes over what he should do and eventually decides to act.
9. He seeks the help of another bishop, who advises him to be careful.
10. He's disillusioned – no-one seems to care what has happened.
11. A police detective talks to Bob as part of routine investigation – You were the kid's priest, did he say anything to you about why he'd kill himself? He tells Bob the autopsy report shows that the boy had been abused.
12. Bob must face his worst fears.

13. Another boy turns up – harangues Bob and says he has caused the death of Boy One. He attacks the priest, they fight, priest finally accepts that he must do something.
14. Dilemma – he cannot report to his bishop, because the man has been accused. He cannot leave it in anyone else's hands – must approach the Vatican for help.
15. Is stalled, frustrated, anxious.
16. The second boy is found dead – also an apparent suicide. Police investigate.
17. Bob is threatened in an oblique way by his mentor bishop. Warned to back off, or consequences might be severe.
18. Bob struggles with his conscience. He is called to give his evidence to the Diocesan committee appointed by the Vatican – is afraid to go because he doesn't know how far the rot has spread.
19. Bob gets together with police detective, determined to bring everything out into the open. By this time he believes that his respected mentor and many of his colleagues have been involved in something unspeakable. He challenges the Code of Silence that prevails.
20. Bob is attacked and beaten in the church as he prepares the sacrament.
21. Jolted into action, he uncovers a link between the Bishop's paedophilia ring and organized crime.
22. He becomes discouraged; sure he has lost everything and yet is helpless to bring the wrongdoers to justice.
23. He is visited by the first boy's sister – she expresses her gratitude to him for trying, and asks him to continue to seek justice for her brother and the other boy.
24. He's encouraged (and maybe by this time a little bit in love with this woman). He discovers a piece of evidence that links the Bishop's office to organized crime.
25. He presents the evidence to the police. They raid the Bishop's palace as well as the organized crime bosses' homes. The case is made against the church.

26. Bob is praised by higher-ups in the church, publicly, but privately a colleague voices the opinion that while what Bob did was very brave, it was the wrong way to deal with it. The Church doesn't like to air its dirty laundry in public, the friend says. He suggests that the Bishop and his cronies, like other disgraced priests, would have been put out to grass by the Vatican and the Church would not have been damaged as it has been by Bob's revelations.
27. Bob is disgusted. He realises that he no longer wants to be part of an organization that acts so covertly. After spending some time wrestling with his conscience and praying to God for guidance, he decides he is leaving the priesthood. He feels bereft, although he has not lost his faith. The first boy's sister praises his decision.
28. Ends where there is a suggestion that the two will get together and Bob is leaving to an entirely new and exciting life.

See how brief this is – just ideas written down point by point. But it is more than enough to keep you writing on track, even allowing for changes as the book unfolds. You can read them over, move them around to keep in sync with the chronology and the action, add to them as ideas strike you. Yes, the brief outline is fast, efficient, and workable.

CHAPTER THREE ASSIGNMENTS

Exercise 3:1: Using your logline as a base, add all the other things you've added to your idea for your novel, and then create a brief point-by-point outline.

Exercise 3:2 Using the guidelines above, put together a novel planner notebook.

See which one best suits your working style!

CHAPTER FOUR

HOOK YOUR READER.

In my opinion, this is one of the most important parts of successful story-telling – good writing has a flow that leads your reader on from chapter to chapter, scene-to-scene, in a seamless way.

"I just couldn't put your book down!" is a reader statement that's always music to our ears, and we get that by using hooks and cliff-hangers to make them want to keep reading from scene to scene, chapter to chapter.

This chapter is all about **hook beginnings** and **cliff-hanger endings**, which are used to keep the flow going in your story and keeping the reader, well, 'hooked' into the story. This creates the 'waves' of action-and-rest that help your reader get excited and then take time to digest the story, all the while knowing that the next wave of activity/tension/action will be crashing ashore any moment now! When you begin your book with an intriguing paragraph, the reader wants to find out what it's all about.

The most intriguing first line hook I ever saw was: "I wasn't there when I died." I can't remember the name of the author or the title of the book, but that one line impressed me enough to remember it several years later - and to take the book home.

We've already discussed the idea of beginnings, middles and ends but your book doesn't just have one of each. Each chapter or scene has one beginning, middle, or end - meaning your book could have ten, twenty or more of them.

That's not as daunting as it sounds. You see, beginnings and ends are magical as far as your reader is concerned: they are the promise that keeps her reading from one chapter to the next, maybe even all night until she finishes the book.

And isn't that a wonderful thought, that someone would say to you: 'Your book was so good, I just couldn't put it down...' ?

How do we do this?

We use hooks.

Yep, just like going fishing.

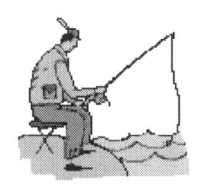

We've already talked about starting at the true beginning of the story, where the excitement is just beginning to build. You can start with something mysterious, exciting, shocking ....something that grabs attention. The first paragraph is usually the clincher for a sale to the reader who has read your back cover blurb and thought she might like to read this book.

Now, you do this with every chapter and every scene if you have more than one per chapter.

A hook is usually short, snappy and intriguing - usually no more than the first two paragraphs. It is written in such a way that it arouses the reader's curiosity, prompting her to read on to find out more. On a more pragmatic note, think of the 'loss leaders' in your local supermarket's weekly advertising flier. The bargain or 'special' lures you into the store, and before you know it your cart is overflowing with other purchases as well!

In our terms, the hook is like a 'special' - it lures the reader in and persuades her that she wants to read the entire book or chapter. Of course, unlike the supermarket's advertising, the rest of the 'goods' you're offering your reader are all high quality and great value!

The middle of your chapter or scene, like the middle of the book, will follow the outline action that you have drawn up. The keyword is motion - keep the story moving along. As you will have seen from the writer's journey, or Hero's Journey, there is a flow to storytelling similar to sound waves through the air - the story starts off on an upward slope to a high tension event, slows down to let everyone catch their breath, then up we go again....with the lows getting slightly higher with each high until the final dénouement at the end of the book, where we tie up all the loose ends and let everyone relax again.

Each chapter starts with a **hook,** flows through the middle, and ends with a **'cliff-hanger'.**

The term "cliff-hanger' dates back to the old black and white movies - does anyone remember The Perils of Pauline? We've probably all seen references to these early adventures, although my guess is most of us are a bit too young to have seen them first run-through!

Pauline was the heroine in a series of movies where she went through many trials and tribulations. At the end of each movie Pauline was left in dreadful straits - tied to the tracks in front of a speeding train, hanging over a steep cliff by her fingertips, trapped in a runaway car speeding towards a flooded river……..

Each week faithful fans returned to the movie house to find out how Pauline was rescued from the latest terrible situation; and, of course, she was always rescued - she had to be back in her starring role the following week!

That's what we call a cliff-hanger ending. You can probably already see why one of these at the end of each chapter would seduce your reader to glance at the first page of the next chapter to see how it all worked out - and the hook at the beginning of that chapter will keep her reading towards the next cliff-hanger....the next hook....and on into the wee small hours of the night!

It's a crafty way of keeping the tension up and drawing the reader more deeply into your story. The hook that follows a cliff-hanger does not necessarily have to be the segment of story immediately following the cliff-hanger - or the bit where Pauline is rescued. You can go to another thread of the story, but you must use a hook so the reader continues reading seamlessly as she knows she is being led to the moment when all the threads are pulled together at the end.

One caveat, however. The cliff-hanger ending does not apply to the very end of the book. This is where all the reader's questions are answered, and while your characters may not be guaranteed a happily ever after, they are at least generally out of danger, emotionally on solid ground again, and ready to get on with the next phase of their lives, having changed for the better due to the events and lessons they learned in the story.

In other words, while the end of a chapter is meant to be exciting and raise questions about what happens next, the final end of the book is calming and answers all those questions.

Once you get into the habit of thinking of your chapters like this, it will come easily to you. Like magic!

We're now ready to start writing the first chapter, so this is as good a time as any to talk about Writer's Block. Few writers never experience that awful moment when the words just won't seem to come, when you think you've lost your writing voice forever. Others declare that writer's block doesn't exist. Once you're writing you can make up your own mind but, like the Dreaded Sagging Middle, writer's block is something I think is worth talking about.

WRITER'S BLOCK – IS THAT OLD BOGEY MAN HIDING UNDER YOUR BED???

Remember when you were a little kid, and you were afraid to get out of bed in case the monster that lived under there grabbed you? I'm sure you do – you're a writer, and writers are born with active imaginations. Your childhood was probably peopled by characters both human and fantastical who were as real to you as if they actually existed. And some of them were probably genuinely scary.

Just like Writer's Block.

And you were probably **genuinely** scared, experiencing that heart pounding, no-one-can-save-me-now feeling you get when you sit and stare at the blank screen, absolutely sure the Writer's Block monster is going to grab you and drag you down to....well, you probably have your own ideas of the scary place those monsters take little kids.

BUT – the whole point of this is that Writer's Block is exactly like the monster under your bed – it's scary but really, really it simply doesn't exist. And yes, you're scared, you're really, really scared. But the source of your fear isn't real.

Now, do you feel silly?

Well, don't. You're not the only one to break out in a sweat, convinced you'll never write again. As a psychotherapist, I can tell you I've had clients afraid of stranger things than Writer's Block – and their demons were every bit as real and inevitable to them as your Block seems to you.

Want to know how I can speak so definitely?

Well, it's not some alchemy born of training as a psychologist. Even though that kind of training encourages students to poke and prod at all the monsters in our heads, learning just what particular button to press to make them disappear in a puff of psychic relief. But that's not where I learned the secret about Writer's Block.

No, I learned it from successive news editors at newspapers where I worked for years. News editors – now they are really scary monsters and believe me, they do exist, and their teeth and fangs are real....

And when a deadline looms and your editor yells across the newsroom: "I want 500 words and a sidebar on that (fill in your own blank/topic!) for the front page!" no reporter who wants to live long enough to get a lunchtime, paper's-to-bed beer is ever going to say: *"Oh, Mr. News Editor, I'm sorry but my Muse has left me and I've got Writer's Block, so you'll have to publish with a blank space on page one. Maybe people can use it for a grocery list…"*

Yeah, right. And maybe that reporter can join the ranks of the unemployable.

So, what to do about those times when you just can't seem to write? Well, first of all, drop this idea of Writer's Block. Ever noticed that, when the words of the beast appear in writer's journals and articles, it's always capitalized? We're scaring ourselves, is what we're doing. Creating monsters to excuse the fact that we're simply not doing our job.

There are a number of reasons why we do this:

Fear is the most common. Let's face it, being a writer is a dream most of us have nurtured for a long, long time. And we can go about saying that we're writers, we're going to write a book/article/screenplay, whatever and people will look suitably impressed or insultingly bored, whatever.

And eventually, they'll ask: *Like, when is this going to be published?*

And that's the scary thing at the root of most so-called blocks. Because eventually, if we ever finish our work in progress, we're going to have to send it out into the big bad world. A world that may reject it. What if we don't make it? What if people laugh? What if our stories are old and hackneyed and boring or…..what if we've no talent?

Well, the sad news is that you won't know until you grab that monster by the nose and wring out your story, painful word by painful word, until it's there in all its glory.

Then you'll send it into the world, and start on the next one. And the next. And someday, if you hone your craft, you'll be published. And I hate to burst that glow of hope, but then you'll face Writer's Block's big brother – SecondBookitis: The paralysis that grabs writers of a newly published first book and convinces them that they can't perform the same trick again.

Welcome to the Real World, baby!

Another reason why you can't seem to make your fingers fly across those keys may be that there is actually something wrong with your story. There's a clash between what you're writing and what your brain, or your creative muse, is telling you is right. Sometimes it can be as simple as an implausible scene. Someone's being asked to step out of character, and refusing to do so. You've got an unlikely situation, and it's simply not working, no matter how wonderful it may have seemed when you dreamed it up.

Go back into your work in progress. Read what you have. Research, research, research. Maybe there's something there that you've got by wishful thinking, not by checking facts. Think about it. Take long walks and consider your story – your cardiovascular system and your dog will love you for it. And somewhere around all this, the answers will pop into your head. The plot will right itself, the characters act as they should, and all will be right with your imaginary world.

But dwelling on the idea of Writer's Block will only reinforce your righteous conviction that something is stopping you from writing.

Something is. **You**! As Woody Allen once said: "The only thing standing between me and success is me."

How right that is!

There are a few tricks to deal with writers block. One often recommended it to simply sit and write – anything at all. Gibberish. A grocery list. Stream-of-consciousness jottings that will eventually metamorphosis into something meaningful. That no doubt does work for some people. All it does for me is give me a few pages of depressingly useless nonsense and a headache, but it's worth a try. It could work for you.

My own favourite strategy is to always end my writing sessions at a point where it's easy to pick up and carry on. Some writers stop mid-sentence, or mid-page, mid-chapter. I always stop at the end of a chapter (yes, I write short chapters!) but with the events that will follow very clearly indicated.

In novels where I'm using a Novel Planner Notebook with an overall outline and small outlines for each chapter, I may not keep strictly to the outlines. Something I've scheduled to happen in chapter seven might not occur right then, or even at all – but it means I know where I'm going.

And when I sit down and start writing, the first thing I do (well, after playing several games of solitaire and checking email) is to read the chapter from my previous writing session. I allow my **Infernal Internal Editor** the opportunity to do his thing (I just know my IIE is a male – only a male could be THAT nit-picky!) and correct a few typos or errors.

Then, following the guidelines of the outline, I head off merrily down the path that flows directly from that chapter, marked out in the outline for the next chapter.

That may not work for everyone, but if you've reached the stage where you think you're blocked, it's worth trying anything rather than suffer.
One thing you can be sure of is that the only way to rid yourself of the pain caused by all those words and ideas dammed up in your head is to put them down on paper, or disc, or whatever.

Get the work done. Pour out that story. Write what's in your heart. Polish it and primp it and send it off like a mother sending a child to school for the first time. Weep a little. Be scared!

You know all the dangers that lurk out in the big world that threaten your baby. But that baby needs to be out there – and you know it. So, just get on with it. You'll feel better for it, you know.

Now, repeat after me:
There is no such thing as Writer's Block!

We are writers, and we will write. We will hone our skills – and that involves writing, writing, writing. And that's just what we'll do….we'll reduce the monster to a pretty pussycat!

Lesson Four Assignments

Assignment 4:1: Familiarise yourself with the idea of hook beginnings, hook chapter beginnings, cliff-hanger chapter endings and all-loose-ends tied up final endings.

Take out two novels from your bookshelf at random. Look at the first couple of paragraphs in the book. What is it about them that makes you want to read on?

Look at the beginnings of some of the chapters - what is the hook?

Is there a cliff-hanger ending?

Did the ending of one chapter lead you directly into looking over to the first page of the next - in other words, did it keep you reading?

If the answer's yes, why?

If the answer's no, why?

Can you identify what was lacking? Analyse your reaction to the paragraph.

If you didn't like the first paragraph or two, can you rewrite them to make the hook more interesting?

Assignment 4:2:

Now we're going to roll up our sleeves and start work. We've laid the foundation; now we start to build your novel.

For the next part of this assignment, write a hook opening (one or two paragraphs) for the first chapter of your novel. Remember, the idea is to draw the reader in, capture their imagination and curiosity so they'll keep on reading.

Don't agonize too much - just let your imagination run and see what you can come up with. Think like a reader!

CHAPTER FIVE

In this chapter we look at character building, and getting up close and personal to the main protagonists in your story. I think you will find the character sheets especially useful, although it does take time, patience and thought to fill them out.

Once you know them really well, you will be able to have them behave and react authentically to the situations you're going to throw at them. This is also a powerful weapon against Writer's' Block - one of the reasons for getting blocked in the first place can be a subconscious realisation that you're forcing one or more characters to act in a way his/her personality wouldn't, in order to squeeze him into the storyline.

CHARACTERIZATION.

Very few stories would be complete without characters – I'd say it's just about impossible to write a story without them. Even stories that feature animals have these critters as characters – and stories featuring the elements, and even inanimate objects are invested with some kind of human characteristics in writing about them.

In some cases even the city the story is set in or the weather that batters the characters and frustrates their plans becomes a sort of character in the book. (Remember the famous opening line: 'It was a dark and stormy night…..'?)

So who are these people who populate first our brains, and then our pages?

Often characters spring fully-grown into your mind. You can just about reach out and touch them – or at least call them on the mind-phone. That's great at the beginning of the story, but then the familiarity with the characters can start to fade as we continue along and other characters join in. How to avoid this?

GET TO KNOW YOUR CHARACTERS.

Build them from the ground up, but do it subtly. Let them reveal themselves to you just as a new acquaintance would. You know, you meet someone and they seem really sophisticated and distant. But a couple of meetings later, you realise they have a wicked sense of humour. Maybe that self-assurance isn't more than skin deep. Maybe that cool exterior hides a seething mass of anxieties and neuroses.

That's when you slowly realise that they have a past, a time before you knew them, which has shaped who they are today.

We talk about 'nature/nurture' when we talk about personality development. Did someone turn out the way they did because they were born that way – nature - or because of the way they were treated as children – parenting/nurture?

Most psychologists today tend towards the nurture and nature combination – we are born with certain characteristics, but the way we are treated as a growing being and the events that dominate our evolving catalogue of experiences decides which characteristics are strengthened and which become minor.

For example, a child born with a tendency towards anxiety may well grow to a relaxed, laid back adult if he is reared in a calm, loving atmosphere where his anxieties are soothed and he learns how to control them and, perhaps even more importantly, realises that he is in control of his life.

The same child, however, brought up in a frenetic, unsupportive or dysfunctional household may grow up anxious and insecure, a candidate for compulsive behaviour disorder and numerous other mental health problems. Or he may grow into a volatile, hostile, domineering and violent character who simply loses his cool if the world around him doesn't fall into line.

Because he cannot handle the anxieties that flow in around him and make him feel out of control, he constantly seeks to be in total control, and anything out of the ordinary throws him for a loop.

So, what personality quirks and strengths does your character have? And how did his life so far shape him? When you're really having difficulty with a character, you may need to think right back to his childhood – where did he come from? What was his family like? His schooling? What forces shaped him?
Even the time in history in which we are born affects who we may become – hence the phrase 'War Babies' to describe an entire generation who were a puzzle to their parents.

That can sound quite daunting, but it's not really.

However, another way to handle this is to write down everything you want your character to be – is he an Alpha male? One of those people who have to win at any cost? A company executive at 30 and a heart attack patient at 35?

Or is he a laid back character, one of those kids whose teachers always said 'Could do better if he worked harder?' and 'Not working to his potential'? Think of the ramifications for your story if your character is either one of these, because these characters will behave quite differently in whatever situations you place them. Many books have been written pairing two characters like these in stressful situations and exploring what happened.

A few years ago there was a lot of talk about personality studies and Type A, and B personalities. It was suggested that the ambitious Type A personalities were the company executives and high achievers. Later research has shown it's often not so – Type A's are so anal retentive, volatile and hard to get along with, not to say too caught up in themselves, to be efficient. They may not rise above middle management, and the real powerhouses are actually the milder characters of Type B personalities.

So, build your characters based on the roles they are playing and the way they must interact in your story. Most writers base characters' behaviour, voices, habits, mannerisms, etc., on people they know, have met, or observed at some point.

Remember, though, that all your friends and relatives will be trying hard to identify themselves in your work, so disguise your characters well. Usually they'll be a mixture of the many different people you know, have met, worked with, sat on a bus next to, spent time in the airport lounge with, sat in class with, or seen on television or at the movies.

You can also use magazines to help build your characters – read interviews with celebs and other people who have been written up. Cut out pictures of people who look like your character. Imagine how they'd look with an eyebrow raised, or picking up a baby, or toting a gun, or whatever. Once you've got it right, you've got your character. Make a character scrapbook, or pin these up on a cork board near your workspace.

If you're writing and something doesn't feel quite right, it may be time to stop and ask: *What would my character do? Is this scene so out of character that it's throwing off the whole story theme?*

Remember that characters often seem to have minds of their own, so trying to force them into uncharacteristic behaviours is a great way to spark Writer's Block. Of course, it's not really your character but your subconscious mind that is objecting to the route your plot is taking.

At least, I think so. It would be too creepy to think the character was actually actively influencing the writer. *They ARE imaginary people, aren't they?*

Remember that having a good chat with your characters can sometimes clear the air and clarify what you need to do. It helps make them seem real to you, and that's what we are looking for – real characters. Remember the fun you had with an imaginary friend or a favourite stuffed animal when you were a kid? Try to bring back that feeling with your characters.

Talk to them. Listen to them. Interview them. Just make sure you do this in private. Talking to oneself is acceptable in a writer, but answering oneself back can still cause raised eyebrows. And when you start sending your characters birthday and Christmas presents, you're really in trouble…..

Don't forget to keep a character page for each of the main characters and alongside *the physical details tab* write down all the traits and odds and ends of background information you learn about them. It's a big help when you must decide what they would do in a given situation.

There are a number of books on the market for writers about personality types – check the writers' digest books – www.writersdigest.com and look for books on characters or personality types. Also there are lots of sites on the Internet, such as http://www.humanmetrics.com/cgi-win/JTypes3.asp http://www.selfmasterysecrets.com/knowthyself/ if you want to delve deeper. All were operational the last time I visited. Beware, many of them let you take a personality test, and you can spend a lot of time browsing here!

Instead of just putting your own personality traits into the questionnaires, you can insert the answers you think your character would give and get a Personality Type designation for him or her that will help you develop the character.

Now onto the character sheets (below). Photocopy or print these, or scan into your computer, then fill out the notes as you go along. The character sheets are printed on full pages to make copying them easier so that you can use the sheets for as many different novels as you like.

CHARACTER SHEETS:

Main Character 1:

Name:
Age(including month of birth):
Place of Birth:
Ethnic Background (if important in your story)
Town He/she calls home now:
Info about Family(including parents' occupations and background, brothers, sisters, etc.)

Any important details about family members, i.e. Father won a heroism award, or was an alcoholic, etc.:

Schooling:

Qualifications:

Current Employment:
Previous Employment:

Financial State:

Personal Health:

Main Ambition:

Hopes & Dreams:

Greatest Fear:

Endearing Traits or Habits:
Bad Habits:

Favourite Food/ Beverage:
Least Favourite Food/Beverage:

Favourite Colour:
Favourite Clothes Style:

Relationship with other characters in story, especially the main characters (are they friends, business acquaintances, lovers, childhood sweethearts, married, business partners, etc.?)

Favourite Pastime or Hobby:

Anything else you can think of that is pertinent to this character's role in your story:

PHYSICAL DESCRIPTION:

Hair:
Eyes:
Skin:
Height:
How would you rate him/her in the looks department:
Why would you rate him/her like that:

Does he/she stand straight or stoop?:
Weight:
Wear Glasses or have other sight problems:
Have a limp, squint or any other obvious physical attribute?
Is the character: active, sporty, a couch potato?
Physically fit and toned, just 'normal', or physically unfit, or even unhealthy:

Anything else that affects his/her role in your story:

Chapter Five Assignments

Exercise 5:1: Fill out the extended character sheets for your main characters - you probably only have one or two. Transfer a précis of the main details to the Novel Work Planner.

Exercise 5:2: On the Novel Work Planner, fill in the other character descriptions on here with brief details about secondary characters. They rarely need a full sheet to themselves.

Exercise 5:3: Now consider these characters. Are you satisfied that they fit the roles you want them to play? Do you need to make any adjustments? Remember that these are not written in stone - your characters can and will change in personality, although probably not in physical description, as you get further into the novel.

CHAPTER SIX

This chapter covers **Dialogue** and **Point of View (POV)**. These are two of the major components of writing a good novel – using the power of dialogue to make your reader love your characters and feel for them. You can use just a few lines of speech to add lots of information that would take up pages if used as narrative, and to give **backstory** without it being stilted and boring.

Yes, dialogue is one of my favourite tools!

Also vitally important is the POV – this is the character viewpoint from which your story is told. Choosing the character through whose eyes the story unfolds is a major decision that affects how the story is told, the tone and style. Usually there is one main POV character, but in some genres, such as any of the romance categories, there are two – the hero and the heroine.

You want your readers to identify with the characters, to see the story through their eyes, but you really need to have most of the tale told by one or two main characters. If you flit around between everyone's point of view, it might seem fair but we're not running a democratic election here.

No, we want the reader to see the story through the eyes of the person/persons most involved. Your hero, your heroine.

There is a place for the POV of secondary characters, when they can add something that's not available from your hero/heroine's POV. For example, in mystery stories you often see the bad guy's thoughts in italics as he stalks the hero/heroine. But the main point of view is still the hero/heroine's.

Now, here we are at the exciting point in the book where I'm going to ask you to roll up your sleeves, take a deep breath - and write your first chapter using everything you've learned so far. Take your time and relax over the process. Enjoy seeing your characters come to life!

POINT OF VIEW: JUST WHO'S TELLING THIS STORY ANYWAY?

Point of view is very important in any written piece. Who is telling the story? Whose point of view are we hearing? As in real life, the point of view can affect the interpretation of events – and different characters may have a different 'take' on those events. Each of your characters will tell his or her part of the story in their own distinctive way.

Again, it is good to stay with the POV of only one or two main characters. If you allow every little secondary character to muscle in you'll have a very confusing story.

Remember, your reader sees the events through the eyes of whichever character is telling the story. For this reason, be careful in your choice because the character can only relate events and circumstances for which he or she is on stage at the time. If you choose to work in only one POV, then you can tell the story of events that occur ONLY while your character is present.

If your character can't hear, see, smell, or know what is going on, then you can't tell it except by having other characters discuss it – that's 'hearsay' as the police would define it!

There are several recognised points of view and, as with most things involving writing, there are different opinions about what they are. Here's my take on the situation:

First Person Viewpoint: This is when a story is written in the first person – 'I'. While it is a useful storytelling tool, particularly for verbal media such as radio or in parts of a television production (think the narration by the dead Mary Alice in Desperate Housewives), using first person can create difficulties on the printed page because it limits what you can tell your readers. You can only tell or describe the actions, events, dialogues, etc., that your POV character can see or experience . Therefore, if your 'I' character is not on stage, you can't relate any action that occurs. Effectively, there is NO action if your character is not on stage!

Although it went out of style, first person is becoming fashionable again in some specific genres. Mystery stories, for example, such as those by Sue Grafton & Robert Parker, or in romances such as those by Mary Stewart or Daphne DuMaurier.

It can also be used in action/suspense, but can make for difficulties when describing physical fights, etc. Imagine: 'He punched me on the nose and I fell down while trying to kick him in the ribs…..' etc. This loses its nerve-wracking tension, doesn't it? If not carefully handled, narration like this loses immediacy and drama and simply reads like slapstick.

Second Person Viewpoint: - 'You'. Sometimes used for children's books. 'You' is rarely used for any other form because it is so limited and makes for very clumsy writing. In non-fiction you can use 'you' to describe something someone can do – for example, in a travel piece, you might say: 'In Jamaica, you can dance all night to the beat of the steel drum band.' But you would not use 'you' throughout the entire piece; instead you would move on to third person with possibly even a few first person observations thrown in.

Not only is this POV messy and hard for readers to understand, particularly in fiction, but editors generally don't like second person viewpoint.

Third Person POV: He/she. One of the most popular points of view in writing, it still limits you to whatever the character can see, hear, feel, etc. It's fine if your main character is always on stage and always part of the action, but not great if you need to put in information that other people have. You have to do some fancy footwork with dialogue and narrative to keep this POV going.

Omniscient POV: This is the all-seeing point of view – your story is told from every viewpoint but it's basically the author telling the story. You can throw in things that your characters couldn't possibly know, including future events. *'Little did Jim know that next week he was going to find his true love and win the lottery.'* Not only does this style interfere with the flow of the story, taking the tension and suspense away, but it creates some interesting problems with past, present and future tense.

Worse, this POV tends to hold the reader away from the characters, stops them 'bonding' with the hero or heroine and their buddies. Popular in Victorian days – Dear Reader type of thing - but not really popular any longer. Omniscient POV is a bit like television sports coverage – all angles at once. Fine for football, but clumsy and awkward, not to say confusing, for written stories.

Dual or Multiple POV: This is the most frequently used and definitely the most workable for modern writing. Dual or multiple POV involves telling the story from the viewpoint of the character best suited to tell it at any one time. For example, you may have a scene where you need the hero's and the heroine's viewpoints to make the scene well rounded and complete.

Watching Zoe, Cliff could see she was making up her mind. His stomach clenched with worry.
Zoe felt Cliff's eyes on her. Should she tell him what was on her mind about their last date? She knew he was anxious, but was so afraid he wouldn't understand..

In this way, we can use both characters to build tension in the story and to convey information that moves the story along.

The big thing to remember with POV is don't **'head-hop'**. Always make your POV changes clearly in a way which your reader can follow. Never force your reader to flip back to the previous paragraph or previous page to figure out who is 'speaking'. Some writers argue there should be no more than one POV per scene; certainly I'd say no more than two POV changes per scene and then using only the main characters. More than that and you're going to have your readers thoroughly confused. If they have to turn back a page or more to clarify whose POV is which, then you're in trouble.

I've been told I tend to unfairly favourite dual POV's in this lesson, so I'll repeat again: Your writing is your writing, and the final choice is yours!

EXAMPLES:

First person: I murdered Jack with a sledgehammer
Second Person: You murdered Jack with a sledgehammer
Third person: He/She/It murdered Jack with a sledgehammer
Omniscient: Jack will be murdered by a sledgehammer wielded by…..
Dual: He murdered Jack with a sledgehammer. Jack saw the hammer raised above his head, and heard Carrie screaming.

See how much more you can say when you use the dual POV?

Betty was so angry. She glared at Jim. Her face was red and her emerald eyes were flashing – **wait! This can't be told in Betty's POV – she can't see herself so how can she say her emerald eyes are flashing?**

Betty felt her face grow hot. She knew she must be beet-red with anger. She pushed her hair back from her forehead in a furious gesture.
Jim saw the fury in Betty's emerald green eyes - they flashed with anger and he knew he was in trouble! – **Reads better, yes?**

First Person:
I walked onto the railway bridge, and saw Sarah at the other end waving at me. I waved back. I could hear her shouting.

Second Person:
You walked onto the railway bridge. You saw Sarah at the other end. You could hear her shouting.

Third Person:
He walked onto the railway bridge. He could see Sarah at the other end. She was shouting. He could see a train behind her.

Dual POV:
Jim walked onto the railway bridge. He saw Sarah at the other end. Sarah waved to Jim, her heart beating frantically. "Get out of here, Jim," she shouted. "There's a train coming!"

Again, see how much more we can get into the story by using two POV's? In the example above, if we could only say that Jim was on the bridge and could see Sarah waving, the reader would have no idea why. Not, until Jim finally saw the train arriving. Switching to Sarah's point of view, we seriously increase the tension by letting the reader know that danger is rushing towards our hero!

DIALOGUE: HE SAID, SHE SAID……..

Point of view and dialogue are closely related, so we're going to deal with them both in this chapter.

Dialogue, Narrative & Exposition

Writers use different ways to get information across – **dialogue, narrative, and exposition.**

Dialogue **is the stuff your characters say (exterior dialogue) or think (interior dialogue),** usually found in speech marks or italics. Dialogue is immediate; it is what your characters are thinking or feeling as the story unfolds. It helps strengthen the reader's sense of participating in the story and helps the reader become attached to the characters and care about them. It is also a vehicle for putting across information and backstory.

Narrative **is the action of the story,** describing what your characters are doing or what is happening to them and how they respond. Again, narrative action is immediate, and told through the eyes of the character's POV. The reader is more likely to believe the narrative, so make sure that narrative and dialogue support each other. However, clashes can be used to create tension and suspicion – if your character says one thing and does another, it raises questions about his/her motives and character integrity.

Exposition **is information you give the reader directly**, i.e., statements from the writer, not through a character. This tends to make the writing flat and robs you of opportunities to add texture and involve the reader.

You can say as the writer in exposition: *Jack had always loved Emma.* This is what we call telling, not showing – ***remember the old writing admonition to 'show, don't tell'*** – in that you are giving the reader information and asking them to take your word for it. But by doing so you are taking them out of the 'now' of the story and losing a valuable tool for enhancing your characters through their own actions and POV.

Anything that interrupts the flow of the story is definitely undesirable as it will shake your reader out of your book's world and, once distracted, you may not be able to lure her back. You leave your reader wondering why Jack has always loved Emma, why his actions aren't demonstrating it, and what evidence there is that this is so.

Instead, you can include this evidence by having Jack look at Emma with love in his eyes, addressing or touching her with a familiarity that shouts love! Doing something nice for her, having his heart leap at the sight of her, etc... ***In other words, get this information across in the character's point of view, rather than from the writer.***

Another problem with making a statement like the one above is that your reader has no input into it, and reader interaction – when your reader is involved and interpreting the story in her own way – is one of the hallmarks of a good story.

But if the writer makes statements, he or she robs the reader of that interaction. She can't say ***well, maybe Jack is only pretending to love Emma,*** **she can't say** ***Jack's really a twisted beast who wouldn't know what love was if it bit him on the nose.*** She's been told by the ultimate authority – the writer – that Jack loves Emma, and she'd better believe it. This takes a lot of fun out of it, and takes away the opportunity to play around a little – maybe Jack really is a twisted beast and you want to drop little clues into his behaviour that show he's not the true lover he pretends to be. Readers like a sense of interacting, of being able to say ***Ah, yes, I knew that Jack was no good!*** Etc.

Keeping the reader guessing, reading the signs, looking for clues and trying to second guess events – and maybe getting them wrong – adds a lot to your story in terms of depth and interest, and reader interaction.

Exposition was very popular in Victorian days, being carried to the extreme of ***"So you see, Dear Reader, Lucy's heart was truly broken...."*** or whatever. But it's very much passé these days.

In **narrative** passages, you can give simple descriptions of people, places, and things. But if you can describe them through your character's eyes, so much the better. Example:

> *The first time she saw Dublin's giant stainless steel spire, it immediately reminded her of the sharp metal spike on her editor's desk, the one he used for 'spiking' articles that wouldn't be used. That very morning he'd spiked her article about corruption in the highest offices of the country, and this act of contempt had ripped through her heart the way the shiny, deadly spike had ripped through the paper.....Now, watching the busy morning traffic on O'Connell Street reflected in the shiny stainless steel sides of the Spire, Lucy vowed that she would continue to work on the story.*

Here we describe the landmark in Dublin city, known locally as The Spike, which tells the reader the story setting, and use it to give the reader quite a chunk of information about the character and about the city. It's not just a description of a monument; it serves to set the story in place, set the time of day the action is happening. It tells us the POV character is a reporter, that she's working on a story about corruption in high places, that her story has been spiked by her editor (and we can surmise this is on the orders of a higher authority) but that our heroine is made of stern, idealistic stuff and intends to continue her investigation despite the setback.

Dialogue is also a wonderful tool for introducing information without long and wordy passages of exposition that would lose your reader. Dialogue can be used to move the action along, inform the reader of **backstory** (details of events that have taken place before the start of your story yet have some influence on the story events), explain the character's actions, show their feelings, and show their character traits.

Never, ever, use dialogue in the same way you might chitchat to the person next to you in the supermarket queue. Like every word in your story, dialogue should have meaning and should take your story ahead.

EXAMPLE:

"Would you like a cup of tea?"
"Yes, please."
"Would you like sugar?"
"Yes, please."
"Would you like milk?"
"Yes, please."
"Did you murder my sister?"

Okay, the last sentence comes as a shock, doesn't it? But the earlier ones are so pedantic and banal that your reader might not make it to the juicy bit. Try this way:

Steve poured two mugs of coffee, holding one out to her.

> *Kelsey struck the mug from his hand, snarling: "Did you kill my sister?"*

Straight to the point, but the action says a lot about the characters and situation: offering hospitality can be construed as a conciliatory act; knocking the mug from her host's grasp is definitely NOT conciliatory and shows a lot about Kelsey's frame of mind and her attitude towards Steve.

Dialogue is a perfect vehicle for backstory:

EXAMPLE:

> *Ted handed her a wad of tissues. "Kelsey, everyone's worried about you. I know you've been upset since your sister died, but isn't it time you pulled yourself together? You can't go around accusing people of murder."*

What do we learn from the above piece of dialogue?

* Kelsey's sister has died recently.
* Kelsey is still very upset.
* She believes someone murdered her sister.
* She's investigating.
* Her friends are worried about her.
* Ted is very concerned about her.
* Ted is close enough to her to be able to speak to her like this, so possibly he is her boss, a close friend, relative, or lover.

See how much information we're able to get in using dialogue? To put this backstory, etc., in as narrative would take several paragraphs, whereas it's very immediate as dialogue and moves the story along without interrupting the action.

In all your writing, you should make every word earn its keep - no flabby sentences or superfluous words. Readers will love you for it. Also, your future publisher will have one eye on costs, and to him/her, extra words and pages cost money so tight **good** writing is a plus.

Obviously your own writing style will influence your use of words, but try to make every word count. And remember Stephen King's advice if you have a particular word, phrase, paragraph, scene that you really, really like but know in your heart doesn't really fit in this chapter or even this book: **'Kill Your Darlings'**.

Edit the words out. Cut and paste them into another file on your computer, labelled 'bits' or some such, where you can keep all these little gems safe until you find the right home for them.

CHAPTER SIX ASSIGNMENTS:

Exercise 6:1: I know, I know, I promised that all the Assignments would be related to your own work, but heck, I'm a writer. I tell lies for a living! Anyway, here are some Assignments you might like to try, just for fun, to test out your dialogue muscles. Imagine each situation and write the dialogue to go with it:

1) John wants Lucy to elope with him, but she's not so sure.

2) Mrs. Griggs always tells her cat about her day, and today was special because not only did she have a visitor – the nice man from the utilities company who spent a lot of time checking the radiators upstairs – but her jewellery box has gone missing from her bedroom and she can't imagine where it is......

3) Right in the middle of Valentine's dinner, Peter tells Susan he wants a divorce.

4) On their honeymoon, Marie has just discovered a photograph of a young boy with the words: **'To Daddy, with Love'** in her new husband's jacket pocket. Simon must explain to her that he was married before and has a son......

Okay, that was a nice break - back to your own project:

Exercise 6:2: Think about your story. If you've started writing, have you chosen the best POV? Whose eyes are you going to let your reader look through? Once you've made this decision, and flexed your writing dialogue muscles, it's time to roll up your sleeves and get down to work.

Exercise 6:3: You have your title, your genre, your opening hook, you know your characters very well, and you have an outline of the main events in your story. You know who's telling the tale. So, get on and get writing!

Open a new document, put your name and contact information single spaced in the top left hand corner. Then centred in the middle of the page, in bold type, write your title, with 'a novel by (your name) ' centred underneath. On to the next page, insert page numbers and using that autoformat space alongside the number, write the title of your book with a hyphen and your name.

Drop down seven lines, and write: **Chapter One.**

Using double spaced lines, write in your hook opening.

Then write that first draft of your first chapter.......and go on as much as you can. Remember that the story should start at the beginning - when the action starts. Don't weigh your beginning down with backstory, but if it's needed, weave a few hints of the past through your characters' eyes and through setting, dialogue, etc.

A chapter usually has at least one scene, which is like a mini-story in itself. You start with your opening hook, something that your hero/heroine must face. Then the middle where she handles whatever the problem is as best she can, and learns something new that helps lead to the conclusion of the story. Then there's the moment when everything in the scene seems resolved, and we're heading for peaceful waters.

Then the cliff-hanger ending of the chapter where we throw a new spanner in the works, or alternatively, add another problem to that growing pile already faced by your protagonists.

So, each chapter has a mini-story, a beginning, middle and ending that segues right into the next chapter.

You are writing. You are a Writer. Isn't that exciting?

CHAPTER SEVEN

This chapter is about **story settings**. As in so many aspects of writing, there's **'micro'** (small, detailed) and **'macro'** (large, overview) settings to work with. Used well, they add a great deal of texture and believability to your work - sometimes the setting can actually become a 'character' in your novel! This is especially noticeable in movies – "Collateral" comes to mind, where the wonderfully descriptive camera work makes the setting a key part of the story.

Setting descriptions should be woven into your story, if possible as part of the action rather than being introduced in pages of 'purple prose'. For example, picture a scene in an outdoor cafe. A couple sitting at a table, he pulls out a cigarette packet and she immediately moves the ashtray from their table to another table - what does this tell you about the couple? Perhaps they don't know each other well, she doesn't like smoking, he can't give it up, and moving the ashtray is her way of politely telling him so. Or they know each other well and she's concerned for his health and is trying to make him quit.

Or, on a deeper level, perhaps she is a very controlling person and moving the ashtray is a power move - the reality would be clear in context, but it also allows you to describe the setting in an active way, the description doing double duty in telling something about your characters rather than being a simple escription......right? In modern writing, every word must earn its keep.

You can use settings to get across a lot of information about your story – e.g., the description of a crime scene, or the particular location such as a tornado-prone area. Or it can be applied to the characters - do they live alone in a remote cabin or in a trendy condo downtown? Are they tidy? Do they have lots of photographs of family/friends/personal triumphs? Ashtrays? Hobby materials lying around? Empty glasses?

Have fun working out your settings, and furnishing them!

GETTING IT ALL TOGETHER:

So how do you make this setting stuff work for your own story? By now you know a lot about your characters - remember the character sheets we put together? And you know where you have set the story.

For the Macro Setting, you may need to do some research unless a) the setting is a geographical place you know well or b) you're creating a fictional place.

If you're using a real place that you're not familiar with, try and visit and spend a day or so there, exploring. If you can't do that, go online and search for information about the place See if you can get maps, climate information, architectural descriptions, and culture/social information. Visit your library and see if there are any books on the area. Talk to anyone who may have been there - don't forget to ask on your internet lists (you do belong to some Internet writers' lists, don't you?)

By now you're probably thinking: *So much work, all this research? What's with this climate information then? Has she totally lost it?*

Well, no. I believe we should all learn by others' mistakes. There are many, many stories about writers who've been embarrassed (to put to mildly) by making a mistake because of poor research. One that springs to mind about a geographical location is the story about the writer who had heard about the desert that dominated one of the US states. What the writer didn't know, because he/she didn't research properly, was that most states encompass a large land area.

Just because the one part of a large land area is desert or semi-desert, doesn't mean that another part can't be lush farmland. Not researching properly, the writer used a desert setting in an area many of the readers recognised as actually being dense forest and rich pastureland.....very embarrassing.

Believe me, readers are very quick to write in to you and your publisher to point out the mistakes they find in your books - and they will tell their friends and relatives, too!

So, avoid embarrassment by careful research. If you need to, get in touch with the tourist agency for the area you're planning to use, or even contact the local municipal government offices. People are very helpful when you ask nicely.

Now, on to the **micro** descriptions. You will probably have several of these in your book. The ones that really need attention are the ones where most of the action takes place, for example, the main protagonist's home, office or place of work, favourite restaurant, etc.

Think about your character, and see these places through his/her eyes. Is she a thoroughly modern person who'd love the minimalist white living room with leather sofas and glass-topped tables, with the only colour a vivid splash of abstract art?

Or would she go for the Victorian look, with flocked wallpaper and velvet drapes and fussy table coverings, with dark oil paintings on the wall?

Or perhaps a country look, rustic furniture painted with roosters, gingham curtains and plants flourishing everywhere and dozens of pictures of friends and family and folk art stencils covering the walls?

Or perhaps your book is set in a world of your own making, one which is very different from the one we know. Even in so doing, you need to remember that your characters will still need certain everyday things in their settings, even if they are designed and named differently. For example, they'll need a place to call home and the comforts that go with it. A means of getting from one place to another. They'll probably still furnish their spaces with ornaments and mementos, hobby stuff and pets. Keep it logical, keep it consistent.

Give these settings a lot of thought, to the point perhaps of writing descriptions down, or hunting through magazines and catalogues until you find the perfect setting. You may never use all these details, but, like your character sheets, the setting will anchor your story in your own mind.

Why is this all so important? Because you are anchoring the reader in your story by the setting, and you are giving the reader a lot of information - your settings describe who your characters are, what their interests are, what their habits and hobbies are - and their state of mind. A busy household with young children looks different than a singles' condo; a company president's office is different from the data processing pool. It's not just furnishings, it's ambience, too – the feeling that is added by the 'stuff' they choose to display.

Writing a setting description is more than just jotting down a few details about the size of the room and the colour of the settee. You're describing a chunk of your character's life, so make it interesting. Again, don't fall into the trap of pages of descriptive purple prose. Knit your setting details into the story, and let your reader's imagination do the rest.

When you're in the first heat of writing, rushing to get it all down on paper, may not be the best time to be worried about choosing between Aubusson rugs or shag carpeting, but make sure you leave yourself a note in the text to return and describe the setting accurately once you've finished that first draft. I often use a different coloured font so that the spots where I need to check or add anything are readily apparent.

Where are you going to find ideas for all these scenes? As a writer, you probably take in the details of every place you ever visit. Start carrying a digital camera. It doesn't have to be an expensive one - unless you want to start selling pix as well - or use a cell phone with a camera facility. Just take quick snaps, we're not looking for art. Capture that fabulous antique doorway, the busy streetscape, the landscape around a lake. Peer through the furniture store windows and take photos of a settee or cupboard that grabs your fancy. Take pix inside hotel lobbies. Street graffiti. Auctions. Cars. Sidewalk cafes. Unusual architecture. Parades. Everything is grist to the creative mill.

Remember to keep a good excuse at the ready for suspicious security personnel!

Collect catalogues with furnishings in them - Sears is good. Invest in decorating magazines. Magazines and catalogues are also good sources for other things - your characters and the clothes you'll dress them in.

Put together a scrapbook, if you like, or a collage showing the setting and your characters in the clothes you've chosen – remember the paper dolls and their dresses you saw as a kid? Use these pictures to help you describe settings and clothing. Find a model who looks like one of your characters, then find them the perfect home.......create the right setting for them from magazine or catalogue pictures.

You may find you've not had as much fun since you were six years old and playing with blunt scissors and a glue stick!

SETTING THE SCENE:

We all know that **location** is important to our stories - in some instances, it's a vital. But location, the immediate setting in which your characters are interacting, is more than just a physical place. It speaks volumes about what your characters do and who they are. In the lesson on **characterization**, I said that sometimes the place where the action takes place can be a character in the writing, and that's how strong the impact of Where? can be in your story.

You may have noticed by now that everything in writing is like those little wooden Russian nesting dolls; you open one and there's another inside. In conflict you have internal and external; in story you have plot and sub-plot; and characters display such a wide range of motivations, feelings, emotions, needs, that you could almost see yourself as a counselling therapist before you got them sorted out.

So you won't be surprised to learn that the issue of settings is no different. *Keeping it basic, we have what I call the 'macro' setting and the 'micro' setting.*

MACRO SETTING:

This is the general location where your story is set: the broader area such as the country – France, America, Ireland. Added to that is the actual locality: rural village, ice fields of Alaska, Central Manhattan, Tallaght, (Dublin, Ireland) Leeds (Yorkshire, UK).

Looking at the variety of settings available, you can see that the setting is almost a 'character' in your story because of the influence it has. Think of some of the books you've read. The barren, lonely moors of Yorkshire set the mood for Wuthering Heights; Ruth Rendell's Inspector Wexford mysteries work well in a small English town; James Plunkett uses Dublin as an integral part of stories such as Strumpet City; and could The Devil Wears Prada be based anywhere other than New York City?

The rich tapestry of cultural differences, customs, acceptable and unacceptable behaviour, traditions, language, etc., of places means that you can use the place itself to add depth to your work.

MICRO SETTING:

This is like taking a camera from a wide focus (the wider geographical area) and closing the focus in to picture a much smaller area.

Stories can be broken down into 'scenes' a bit like in movies or television. A scene generally is a complete 'take' – say, a conversation or interaction between characters that moves the story along. There are usually one, two, no more than three 'scenes' in a chapter, but you will find your own writing style.

So a **micro setting** is the small area where the scene takes place – it can be a room, a street, a public building, a woodland glade, a gym, a school staffroom, the room where an evening class is taking place, the small home office where a writer toils, a busy newsroom, a public beach……wherever. It is limited only by your imagination and the requirements of your story!

Once you know where the scene takes place, you need to picture it. Let's say you're doing a scene set in a room. Your characters haven't arrived yet. What are they going to see? Close your eyes. See the room. What elements make it up? Is it an office? A living room? A storeroom? A prison cell? Is there a window? More than one window? Big, small? Does it have colourful curtains? Iron bars? Does it look out onto a garden? A busy street? A desert?

How is the room furnished? Is it modern, old fashioned? Whose room is it? Any interior designer will tell you that our rooms reflect our characters, tastes, lifestyles, social class, wealth (or lack of it), interests. Think of a room in your house – what objects are there because you want them to be? Do you have a special chair, a favourite ornament? Lots of photos of relatives and friends? Are there shelves piled high with books? Or is it minimalist, modern, uncluttered…some rooms are so uncluttered you wonder if anyone lives in them at all!

So, consider the room in which you are setting your story. What does it tell you about the characters? What is there in the room that you can use to move the story along and give the reader information about the characters? Is there a smell of cigarette smoke, a dirty ashtray that the owner can self-consciously shift out of sight while the newcomer sniffs and wrinkles her nose in disgust?

Or perhaps that same dirty ashtray can come as a relief to the visitor – a sure sign that smoking is allowed and she is so nervous, she really needs a cigarette. Or perhaps the place smells of lemon oil, applied by the careful housekeeper to beloved antiques, or lavender wax polish, bringing back memories of granny's parlor?

Are there ornaments the characters can pick up, admire or scorn, perhaps throw at each other? A picture of a dead child that a grieving mother can hold for comfort, smoothing her fingers over the glass? Are there collections that give a clue to the owner's interests, such as china dolls or pretty mineral bearing rocks?

Maybe something offbeat, like a shrunken head from New Guinea or a stuffed elephant foot – these speak volumes about the sensitivity of the owner, as well as their traveling history.

Are there plants in the room? Are they flourishing or neglected? Is there dust on the surfaces, dirty cups on the side tables, newspapers and empty pizza boxes on the floor? Is there a sewing machine, knitting, embroidery – will one of your characters use the knitting needle with nasty results?

Is there a cosy fire? Real or fake? How does the room feel – is it welcoming, or is it stiff and cold? Could you go in and put your feet up with a cup of tea, or would you sit on the edge of the chair with your back straight and look forward to escaping the place? Is the furniture comfortably used, or is it covered in clear plastic and obviously not intended for lounging? Or is there a musty, dusty, closed up and deserted feeling suggesting that no-one has been there for a while?

Magazines, books, music CD's, pictures, photos, letters left lying around all give an idea of the character who lives in that room, as well as providing material for your characters to use.

In the sentences below, we have a simple one line action statement, and then we have a second sentence that says lots about the mood, setting and characters. See what we can learn from the settings:

1) Jean looked out the window to the rain outside.

2) Jean pushed aside the heavy velvet curtain and stared through crystal clear glass at the rain-sodden garden beyond, where the last of the summer roses put on a brave show as though trying to hold winter back. *We learn that this is a well-to-do household or at least one that is, or has been, cared for (velvet drapes and crystal clear window glass?) that there is a garden, again probably well-kept (roses) that it is raining, and the time of year is late fall or early winter. Given the weather, this is probably not a location in an area with an extreme climate!*

1)   Jack stood up as the woman came into the room.

2) Jack tossed the magazine back onto the polished table and stood as the woman entered the room – or at least, he tried to. The deep, soft cushions of the sofa didn't want to let him go and he silently cursed modern furniture manufacturers before breaking free at last.
Jack has been waiting a while – he's done some reading. The magazine and polished table again suggest a well-kept home, possibly with a woman in residence (!) and that Jack wants to make an impression by standing up swiftly but is defeated by the modern deep, cushioned sofa! So, the room is probably furnished in a modern style, and Jack may not be a very patient person!

1) How could anyone live like this? Looking around the drab little room, Ann thought it was no wonder Pete had tried to kill himself.

2) The room was small and bleak, with a dull northern light filtering in through broken plastic slats over the window. The floor was awash with newspapers and old take-out food boxes, and empty glasses stood in a sad row on the scratched and dusty surface of the table. A scent of stale beer and cigarette smoke lay over everything. A telephone directory had been used to prop up one of the table's broken legs, but it still listed depressingly to one side. *How could anyone live like this?* Ann picked up a stack of letters and fanned them out – all bills, all overdue. No wonder Pete had tried to kill himself, if he was reduced to this.

Over and above the stark detail of the first sentence, here we learn that Pete was living in poverty, in a small, bleak apartment with a northern exposure, broken blinds on the window, and a broken down table propped up by the phone directory. Pete's state of mind is further communicated by the mess, the lack of pride in place, and the diet of cigarettes, beer, and junk food. A further hint at his predicament is the stack of overdue bills.

Can you see the impact setting descriptions can have, and how much they add to the texture of your work as well as your reader's image of the character?

Consider the micro setting to be a stage where your characters will act out the scenes. All the things on the set are props that can be used to convey feelings, status, interests, to show when a character is playing for time before answering a question, to identify the character who owns the room and their state of mind and interests.

Remember that your characters can also move the story forward by interacting with the setting – staring out the window, picking up an ornament or photograph, flicking through a magazine, helping themselves to a drink, exercising curiosity by examining books and cds.

Consider the background noises. Is there music playing? The sounds of children in the next room or at a playground outside? Traffic noises? Airplanes roaring in to the nearby airport? The steady hammering of construction sounds, or the beeping of reversing trucks? A baby crying? People shouting? A television left on?

You can do the same with a street scene – developing intimacy between the characters as they lean towards each other to make themselves heard above the traffic noises, or pressing together as people crowd past them, stepping to one side to let a mother push a baby stroller past, drop coins in the hat of a street musician, one reaching out to steady the other as he trips over an uneven pavement.

You can use this technique to deepen your stories with any setting. Just make sure you're accurate. If you're describing a garden, make sure the plants grow in the area you're in – or use the scraggly or abundant growth of the plants to tell about the local climate.

> *Janet looked with pity at the stunted, browning leaves of the rhododendrons – the poor things don't do well in a Northern Ontario winter.*

However, as in all things, don't overdo it. Like many other aspects, **Less can be More.** Don't add so much detail to the setting that it overwhelms your writing – the detail should enhance your story, highlight the tension or the mood, not take it over.

Don't get into long exposition – let your characters' behaviour interact with the props to tell the story. Remember that setting isn't just visual – you can use the tactile feel of things, the match or clash of colours, the smell, the atmosphere, and sound, etc., to deepen the setting.

But again, don't overwhelm your reader with the details. Your readers are intelligent and imaginative. In describing your setting, you are giving them the tools to build the scene in their own imaginations. It probably won't look anything like the setting you saw in your mind's eye, but it will work for each of them.

Chapter Seven Assignments:

Exercise 7:1 Walk into a place you know - perhaps it's your own home. Or a place you wish was your home. As you approach from outside, write what you see....then describe the inside.

What do you see? What does it tell you about the person who lives/works/spends time there? If it's a restaurant, for example, what sort of clientele does it appeal to? Just write a couple of paragraphs to exercise those writing muscles.

Exercise 7:2 Now imagine the macro setting for your book.
 a) Where is it?
 b) Why did you choose it?
 c) What impact does it have on your story?
 d) Is it a real place or a designer setting you made up?
 e) If the setting was someplace else, would that change your story at all?

Exercise 7:3 Choose one of your main characters. Where does he/ she spend the most time? Write a paragraph or two to describe the setting through the eyes of ANOTHER character, and say what inferences this character draws from the setting you have chosen for the first character.

For example, if you want to create an apartment setting as 'home' for your heroine, imagine she's invited the hero over for dinner. What does he see, and what does he think the rooms say about the heroine?

Exercise 7:4 You should also be busily writing the rough first draft of chapter two! It need only be a very rough draft, or the 'crappy first draft' as it's often referred to by writers, but you need to get your story down on paper.

You can't edit what you haven't written, so no matter how rough the first draft is, it's your ticket to a clean, well-written, well thought-out final draft.

CHAPTER EIGHT

In this chapter we're going to do some in-depth work with **conflict** – something that's vital to just about any genre you choose to write.

Conflict is the seasoning that spices up your story. Without conflict, there isn't really a story because your characters have no opposition, no challenge, nothing to strive for or work against. These are the things that cause your characters to grow and change throughout the novel.

Conflict isn't people arguing and yelling at each other but rather, in this context, feeling torn and, well, conflicted. They want something, but something externally prevents them from having it. They have a goal, but something in themselves is stopping them from going after it.

First we'll look at **Internal and external conflict** - you need to know what's happening with your characters so that you can write their story with tension. Then we're looking at **research** - something most writers either love or hate. But it's vital in all novels that you know your facts. Even if you're making up your own world, you need it to be plausible.

Some novels require more research than others - you might need to find out more about life in Victorian times than you would about life in your home town in 2012, but you do need to verify your facts. Make notes as you write, so that you know what you need to find out - and don't sweat it, just keep your research to what you need to know for the book. You can write about a shooting, for example, without knowing the history of warfare. You just need to know the best gun for the job, and whether it has a safety catch, is a revolver, automatic, how many bullets, etc.

Then you're going to roll up your sleeves and get to work on the next chapter draft. After that, with your brief outline and your hook beginnings/endings established, there's nothing stopping you - you can sail through to The End!

STIRRING IT UP - SEASONING YOUR STORY WITH CONFLICT.

Conflict is an essential ingredient in any form of creative writing. There's a tendency to think of conflict as something major, like a war, or at least as a stand-up-in-your-face shouting match or an argument, maybe even a fistfight.

It's not.

Conflict is simply the idea that your characters are torn between what they want or need, and something that is stopping them from getting it.

Remember the Russian nesting dolls I mentioned previously, where you open one and there's another inside? It seems just about everything in writing is like that, including conflict.

There are two kinds of conflict, and if you use this as layering in your story, you will find that you have a much deeper texture and interest.

Let's take a very easy example:

Imagine that your hero wants to go to Spain. He simply has to book his ticket and go. If the only thing stopping him going is that he's too lazy to pick up the phone and book the flight, then no conflict. No conflict = boring story.

Imagine he wants to go to Spain, but doesn't have enough money without going into his savings, which he doesn't want to do because it's taken him so long to beef up that savings account. Okay, some conflict there but not nearly enough to make your reader sit up and take notice. We're still in oh-hum land.

NOW: Imagine that the money in the savings account has been set aside for a serious operation his wife needs. They still don't have enough money and the need for operation is becoming more urgent. Our hero knows that if he goes to Spain he may be offered a really good contract that would give them enough money for the operation. If he goes, it could solve their problems. And on a selfish level, he really, really wants to go, and he really, really wants the contract there.

BUT: If he goes, he'll be taking money from the precious fund AND he might not get the job, which creates a bigger problem. He's torn between taking the safe route, getting the money together slowly for his wife's operation, and staying in a job he actually doesn't like any more. Or going to Spain, becoming a hero for amassing a large amount of money in one fell swoop, and getting the job he really wants in a place that interests him.

If he goes and it all works out, everything will be great.

If he goes and it all fails, he'll have taken a chance that has robbed his wife of the operation she desperately needs.

Now there's conflict!

There is **Internal and External conflict.**

Internal conflict is when your character must fight with himself about what action he should take.

External conflict is when something outside himself – a situation, person, thing, event, etc. – stands in his way.

In the above example, let's name our hero Joe. Joe is conflicted externally, because outside circumstances - his wife's ill-health and their lack of cash for her treatment - are putting pressure on him. He knows if he goes to Spain it may or may not solve their problems. The external conflict is whether or not to risk the money in their savings account, knowing the possible ramifications.

But there is also internal conflict – can he justify going after something he really wants - the Spanish contract - when it means someone he loves - his wife - may be put at risk? Can he justify going after this contract in Spain – for a job he'd really like to do – when if he fails, he'll be blowing the money needed for his wife's operation?

This is the dilemma for which there is no simple solution - and your reader will be on the edge of her seat and (hopefully) crossing her fingers that all works out for Joe and his wife.....but knowing there'll be some tense moments because of the conflict situation. And we haven't even got to his wife's point of view yet!

Here's another:

Annie is 38, married for seven years to Andy, 40. Annie wants to have a baby. Andy doesn't want to start a family. Their happy marriage is on the skids….

Annie:

External: She wants to complete their happy little family with a child. But her husband does not want a child and she can't understand why the man she loves, who has always given her everything he could, refuses her this.

Internal: She can feel her biological clock ticking – soon it may be too late to conceive a child and she desperately would like to be a mother. But her husband, whom she loves dearly, does not want to have a child.

Annie wants to remain in the marriage versus Annie wants a child.

Andy:

External: Their life is perfect, just the two of them. Bringing a child into their family at this stage would spoil everything. They would lose their affluent, carefree lifestyle if Annie gave up her job to be a mother.

Internal: Doesn't he make Annie happy enough? Why does she want to bring another person into their relationship? Isn't he enough for her? Would she love the baby more than him? What if his salary is not enough to keep up their lifestyle? What if he couldn't love a child – he'd make a lousy father......after all, his own dad was useless......

Andy wants to remain in the marriage versus Andy does not want a child.

Annie must find out what Andy's opposition is rooted in. In casual conversation with Andy's mother, she discovers that Andy's father never enjoyed his children and left the family home soon after Andy's youngest brother was born.

"I always told Andy that his father simply wasn't man enough to be a father, that he was jealous because I loved the children so much," Andy's mother declares.

Now Annie must confront Andy with this information and persuade him that he will not be like his father, and she will not love the baby more than she loves him. But will understanding this background be enough to solve the conflict?

Here's a very mundane example of conflict, but one that has layers of relationship needs that could lead to the dissolution of several relationships:

Jim has a book he's only just bought, on a topic he finds very interesting. **Jean** sees the book and asks to borrow it. Jim knows he won't get time to read the book that week, so he reluctantly agrees to loan it to her with the proviso that she return it at the end of the week.

Jean loves the book. She doesn't want to give it back because she hasn't finished reading it. And maybe not even then....

Jim wants the book back. He's angry with Jean for breaking her promise.

Jean wants to keep the book and doesn't care that Jim is angry.

External Conflict: Jim wants the book back. Jean won't give it back.

Jim's bigger than Jean. What's to stop him simply taking the book away from her???????

Lily is what, or who.

Lily is Jim's wife.
She's also Jean's best friend.
Lily will be angry with Jim if he upsets Jean over something as trivial as a book, for heaven's sake…..

Now Jim is caught up in internal conflict.
He wants the book back, but he doesn't want to upset Lily.
Lily is conflicted because she doesn't want Jim to be upset, but she doesn't want to lose Jean's friendship. The book doesn't seem important to her. She tells Jim that Jean will return the book when she's finished reading it.

Jim says he needs the book back to read over the weekend – he has only a few hours of free time.

Jean doesn't really care if either Jim or Lily are upset – after all, she's the sort of person who doesn't return books, what can you expect????????

Jean simply wants to keep the book.

But when we dig a little deeper into motivations:

Jim resents the long hours he works that deprive him of the opportunity to spend time learning about subjects that interest him. The book is symbolic of these interests, and his desire to have the book back for the weekend highlights the fact that he has only a few free hours each week.

Jean, if the truth be told, is enjoying making Jim suffer – uh, oh – here's a tasty bit – Jean's actually jealous because she's never been in a committed relationship but Jim and Lily seem to have such a nice marriage. Jean is lonely, and seeks comfort in books. Added to that, having a book borrowed from someone else is symbolic because it proves that she has friends who are willing to give her/loan her things they value.

She also sneakily thinks Lily would spend more time with her if Jim wasn't around, as they were good friends before Jim and Lily married and she does secretly resent the loss of her friend to Jim.

BUT now she's conflicted – if Lily takes Jim's side, Jean will lose her friendship….and then she'll be even lonelier…..

BUT she still doesn't want to give the book back. Books are Jean's friends…..
Jean is now conflicted because she needs the book as a symbolic friend, yet in keeping it she might lose her flesh-and-blood friends…

See how understanding and using the shades of meaning behind conflict can turn even a mundane situation - the borrowing and not returning of a book - into a deeper conflict situation which is far more interesting?

Each of your main characters will have something they need, want, or desire, and something which is stopping them getting it. Make sure there's an internal and external conflict (sometimes they may appear to be the same thing, especially when emotions are involved) and make sure that the stakes are high enough, the problems serious enough, to keep your reader wondering and worrying and cheering the characters on.

RESEARCH, RESEARCH, RESEARCH…..

No matter what you're writing, you'll probably have to do research. Research garners the little bits of authenticity that will make your work stand out from the crowd - to say nothing of saving you from some very embarrassing moments.

It's important to get the facts right, use the right words in the right context, and be sure that if you're using nicknames, you're using the right one – and the right one in a cultural context, too.

For example, a 'hot shot' used to be a business executive type, often the phrase was a slightly derogatory way to refer to someone overly ambitious and self-important. Now in the US, a Hot Shot is a term used for firemen who fight forest fires, etc, and who are heroes – as are all firemen, etc., in that country since 9/11.

Be aware that the emphasis on getting the research right, having all the details correct, isn't just some insecure anal-retentive trait that can be ignored. Your research may produce that one shiny detail that provides the context for your work; it will provide the authority that will make your work stand out on the editor's desk.

These days there is a trend towards 'authentic' and 'expert' writing. You can see it very clearly in 'how-to' books and in creative non-fiction, but it's also there in fiction. Look at the number of writers who write from a standpoint of having been involved professionally in some aspects of what they write about: Patricia Cornwell, Tom Clancy, Kathy Reichs, Thomas Harris, Tess Gerritsen.

Editors, of course, understand that we're not all experts in all fields, particularly if we're writing about specialist procedures. But they do expect to have the details and procedures correct – that's where research comes in.

Learn about computers if you've a character who works with them. Ditto about horses, dogs, embroidery, television, whatever your characters are involved in, if it needs to be in the book, you should know about it. That's not to say you need to get a doctorate before you can write the book; what I'm saying is you need to know enough to write comfortably and accurately about the things your character is doing.

Given enough time for research and interviews, as well as access to specialists and academic information, a competent writer can drum up a workmanlike essay or article on anything from bread making to nuclear fusion – or use these things to add realism to a fiction story without getting the details wrong.

There is no shortage of information out there – mostly, it's a question of knowing where to look. Information comes mainly in three different forms – hands-on, where you get actual real-life experience of your subject; primary sources, where you get information from interviewing the experts, or people who do have hands-on experience; and secondary sources, where you get information by reading true stories, textbooks, periodicals, biographies and autobiographies, articles, etc.

Hands-on information can come from your own training, work experience, volunteerism, etc. Learn how to shoot a gun, volunteer at the local hospital for medical experience and atmosphere, help out in school classrooms for experience in teaching and the educational system. Take classes in pottery if you need to know the technicalities of throwing pots on a wheel and how it feels to have your hands in that wet clay. This type of research is as much about the visceral as about the dry facts.

Primary sources: You don't have to be a famous author to get people to give you an interview or answer your questions. Most people are quite pleased to share their specialist knowledge and most also get hot under the collar when they see inaccurate details of their own field in books or articles. Phone or write, explain what you are doing and ask if they'd be willing to answer some questions for you.

Tell them you want to be sure to get it right, and few people will refuse an interview.

However, accept that they may be very busy and have to say no, or be tied to a contract themselves and not able to help you without getting permission from someone else. Occasionally you'll meet an expert who's been 'burned' by a bad experience with a writer, and they'll say no to everyone after that. But that's rare. If someone says they don't have time to talk to you, ask if they can suggest someone who might. Then you can use the name of the first person as an 'in' to persuade the next person on your list!

Most organizations, including the police, etc., have public relations departments whose job it is to be helpful to the public – that includes you. Don't be afraid to ask – you'd be surprised how often they get queries from writers.

You might be able to get an introduction through a friend who has a friend who knows someone, and that's fine. But cold calling – calling someone who hasn't a clue who you are – is perfectly all right even if it does take a bit of nerve! Journalists do it all the time – and so do real estate salespeople! Always be polite, rehearse before you call so that you know exactly what you want to ask so that you're not wasting anyone's time.

Be prepared for the person to ask you to set a time for the interview, either by phone or in person, or perhaps to ask for a list of your questions to be faxed or emailed to them ahead of time. This gives them an opportunity to make sure they have enough time to talk to you, to think about what you're asking and have the answers beforehand, especially if you're asking for a lot of technical or specialist information.

Never be afraid to ask your interviewee to recommend the name of someone else you could speak to if they can't answer all your questions, or if you need still more information in a related area. Then you can go to the next person and say 'Mr So-and-So recommended that I speak to you.' That's a good ice-breaker.

Don't grill your interviewee. You're not an investigative journalist hot on the trail of a major expose. Remember, the person you're talking to is a professional – you are one, too. Respect that. Be appreciative of their giving you the time and treat them with professional courtesy. You're a writer who needs facts, figures, and procedural details to make a story work. If they're facilitating your work, then treat them politely and remember to thank them. You never know when you might need to call them again!

Of course, if you do happen to come across an idea for a news story or feature, don't ignore it – you might be able to sell it and at the same time gain some exposure for yourself and the book you're working on.

Be careful if you want to include a person's name in your non-fiction book or article – or in the credits at the front of your book. Whatever the genre. Some people don't want their names made public – this is particularly true of people in the police, for example, or the medical profession. Ask them, and respect their wishes. If you don't, you can kiss goodbye to any future help from them – or their colleagues (word travels fast).

Make sure you mention to the interviewee that you might need to call him/her back. You'd be amazed how, even after a thorough interview and well-prepared questions, some detail crops up as you're writing and you need to get back to the expert for clarification. Once they know you, they may agree to trust you with their email address, if you don't already have it, so that you can whip off a quick email, thereby using less of everyone's time.

When you approach someone for an interview, always be pleasant – imagine how you'll feel in the future when your writing takes you to celebrity status. Won't you want to be treated politely and thoughtfully? Treat your sources in the same way. And don't apologise for your unpublished or little published status. The fact is that you are a writer, you're writing, and you want some help with the details. The very fact that you're willing to research means you're serious and professional – and they'll treat you that way.

Secondary sources of information and research are all around you and, thanks to the Internet, even if you live in Outer Lesser Miggleswade, you'll have access to some of the finest sources in the world. Put in keywords to one of the large search engines - Google is my own favourite – and you'll reap lots of web sites with that information on them. You'll also get lots of sites that don't fit your needs, but it's still a lot easier than searching library card catalogue files and then searching through the shelves for books – and still finding that the references aren't what you want. The Net lets you do research from your own office chair, still in your jammies and bunny slippers if you like.

Visit web sites that look promising, and make a note of the ones that have information that you want to use, in case you need to credit them. Check if the site has a proviso that you have to get permission to use the information. The best thing is to email the people involved and ask your questions that way.

The web can also bring a whole world of books to your door – books you might otherwise have to travel many miles to find, or order from your local bookstore and wait until they arrive. Amazon.co.uk or .com, and other online big bookstores will let you do a search for your subject, then read the 'blurbs' about the books to see if they have what you want. They may also let you return books (unread and unmarked) that turn out to be wrong for what you're looking for.

You'll also find textbooks, the same textbooks the experts use in training, but they do tend to be expensive so be absolutely sure that you'll be using them a lot before shelling out that kind of money. The flipside is that they can give you amazing insights into the way these professionals work and the demands their job makes on them.

You can also join writers' lists online as well as specialist lists for specific subjects – I belong to a forensics science list that is for, well, you guessed – forensic scientists. Learned lots of yummy things about decomposition, blood spray, etc. You may laugh, but it is authentic information straight from the specialist's mouth, and they'll answer questions from innocents like you and me. Sensible ones only, please.

I'd like to quote writer Lisa Gardner in closing: "Just because you've learned it doesn't mean you get to use it." In getting into the minds of your characters you'll learn lots and lots of things – things that help you understand him/her and their work or their motivations. But you won't necessarily need to put all those details in your writing. Too much information, no matter how authentic, will leave your work reading like a textbook and your reader yawning and looking for another book.

Lesson 8 – Assignments

"If I lose the light of the sun, I will write by candlelight, moonlight, no light. If I lose paper and ink, I will write in blood on forgotten walls. I will write always. I will capture nights all over the world and bring them to you." - Henry Rollins

Exercise 8:1 Think carefully about each of your main characters, analyse the part they are to play in your story. We've talked about motivation - now write down the conflicts that each of them faces. Put yourself in the analyst's place, get each character to lie down on your office couch and ask them to tell you how they feel, one at a time, of course!

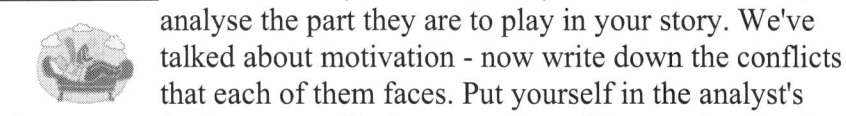

Get them to talk, and whittle out the internal and external conflict. Don't take it on face value. Look behind the obvious to find the psychological/emotional reasons that they have these issues.

This is a good test of how strong your story idea and characters are, and what you will need to do to make them - and their actions and reactions - realistic.

Write your conclusions down in a couple of paragraphs for the two main characters; add to your outline or novel notebook.

Writing Exercise 8:2: Write Chapter Three's first rough draft! It need only be a very rough draft, or the 'crappy' first draft' as it's often referred to, but you need to get your story down on paper.

Remember, you can't edit what you haven't written, so no matter how rough the first draft is, it's your ticket to a clean, well-written, well thought-out final draft.

CHAPTER NINE

In this chapter we look at **Motivation** - why your characters are doing what they're doing - and the **Dreaded Sagging Middle** - not the one you get from spending too much time on the computer with only your fingers doing the exercise, but the one your story gets when the pace starts to slow down after chapter three and you begin to feel the enthusism slipping away.

Motivation is a funny thing - we all react differently to situations because of our past experience and our personalities. In the same way, we all want different things, or the same thing for different reasons....like the poor kid in school who works like a demon because a university scholarship is a way out of poverty, compared to the rich kid who works like a demon because everyone in her family is an over achiever and she doesn't want to let the side down: same goal, different reasons.

Alternatively, there's the really bright kid from a disadvantaged family who is disruptive in class and does no work because he knows he has no chance of getting ahead no matter what because of family circumstances, and the rich kid who is disruptive and does no work because he knows he'll get ahead no matter what because of family circumstances.

Some of us are competitive and need to achieve goal after goal. Some of us are defeated before we reach the first hurdle, and give up. Why? A mixture of personality traits, background, and past experiences.

Then we can go deeper: the abused child who goes on to accept abuse in her adult relationships. Or the abused child who goes on to abuse his partners.

Are they each, in their own way, seeking to validate the

behaviour they witnessed in their parental role models? Is it learned behaviour? A defective gene? Why is one child in a family motivated to do well, one motivated to do all the wrong things? And what effect do these positive and negative experiences have on their behaviour?

As you can tell, the questions of personality, motivation, and the Nature/Nurture question are fascinating. As a writer, you should consider all these aspects of your characters' personalities so that their motivations - and the way they achieve them or act them out - fit with their personality and lend authenticity to your story.

MOTIVATION - ASKING WHY?

We've looked at characters and the conflict that you must throw at them in order to create a story. That's only one part of the puzzle, though. Your characters have to be motivated to act in the ways your story demands.

One way to determine motivation is to play the What If? game. Now, you might think that some of this applies only to fiction writing, not to personal essays or to non-fiction. But all forms of writing involve characters, real or imaginary, and to paint them well in your writing you need to understand them, who they are and what makes them tick.

For example, I once had a student who wrote about her father and his attitude to shoes. He always bought good leather shoes and each day they were polished to a gleaming shine. Why? Because when he was growing up, his family could not afford shoes for all the children. Now, although of modest means, he buys the most expensive quality shoes he can - and he takes care of them for two reasons: 1) because he is very proud of owning the shoes, and 2) because the child in him isn't sure when he'll ever be able to afford new ones.

It is important to understand that everything we do springs from a motivation that we may not be consciously aware of, but which is very strong and prompts us to behave in certain ways.

Indeed, motivation can explain much behaviour which, on the surface, may seem odd. It can also give depth to behaviour which may seem quite ordinary but, like my student's father's shoe shining, has deeper significance.

There is a device used in training journalists - the five w's: who, what, where, when and why? All these questions should be answered in order to have a good, well-rounded story, whether fact or fiction. In this lesson, we're dealing with the Why?

See these examples:

A dog *(who)* ran across (what) the road *(where)* yesterday. *(When).* Yawn. That's pretty boring. The Why? Is missing.

Now see this:

A dog ran across the road yesterday chasing the man who'd just mugged his owner.....

Now, see how the addition of that little why makes it all so much more interesting!

Motivation and characterisation and conflict all go together. Everything your character does is a reaction to events, based on his personality and past experiences. For example, someone who is very confident and is from a safe, secure background reacts a whole lot differently to a setback than someone who has never had money or family support, has no backup systems and has a lot to lose.

Let's look at how you can change to story by changing the motivations.

Imagine a company - let's call it "RipOff Productions" - is about to fold. Meet our cast of characters:

Bill Dwyer is the company CEO. He was thinking about retiring anyway, and is looking forward to getting the golden handshake earlier than he'd expected.

Rosemary Dwyer, Bill's wife, is pleased her husband won't be under the stress and strain of running a company any longer. She's been worried about his health, and thinks perhaps they can travel as they'd always planned.

Lucy, Bill's secretary, is sad at the idea of losing the job she loves and has done for years and wonders what will happen to her, without a job or visible means of support.

Jackie the tea boy – he's worried and depressed because he has no qualifications and little chance of finding another job.

Lizzie, the office manager, whose husband owns his own car dealership, shrugs and thinks she'll have to persuade her husband to pay for her facelift, after all.

Peter, who just got married and took out a mortgage, is probably the worst hit - his wife gave up her job when they moved to the area so that he could take the job with RipOff.

Fred, the caretaker, is just a year away from retirement and worried that he'll lose his company pension.

Superficially, they all react according to their circumstances. But we can shake that up a bit. This is where we play the What If? game -

What if the company director, Bill, has been embezzling and knows that the auditor will look at the books closely now the company has folded? He's not looking forward to retirement; he's panicking at the thought of jail……

Rosemary may actually be dreading the loss of her freedom when her husband is retired and home all day. Her round of coffee mornings and lunches with the ladies may be over. As may her lazy afternoons with the young and handsome gardener…

What if Lucy the secretary has been having an affair with Bill and expecting him to divorce his wife and marry her? Will she try to blackmail him into marriage by threatening to tell about his crooked dealings…..?

What if the Jackie the tea boy doesn't give a damn because he just won the $3.5 million lottery?

What if Lizzie was planning to leave her abusive husband and this job was a means of squirreling some money away to get away rather than just providing a bit of extra cash to spoil herself with? Will this closure prompt her to pack up and leave her husband, or will she resign herself to many more years with a bully? Or will she slip rat poison into his morning tea?

What if Peter's new wife is the daughter of a very rich family who hate Peter and attempt to use this to break up the marriage? Or will his wife be relieved that they can move back to the area where they used to live, and she'll get her old career back?

And Fred, the janitor - will he and his wife decide to spend their savings on that cruise they've wanted so long, or will Fred discover that he's got no pension because the boss embezzled the pension fund, and the shock of job and pension loss results in a heart attack? Or will Fred take his sweeping brush and beat his boss's brains out?

Do you see how the storylines can emerge – and what a difference motivation makes?

It's important to avoid stereotypes. People are complex beings and nothing ruins a good book more than putting obvious motivations onto clichéd characters.

Don't let appearances fool you. For example, let's think about a character named John. John comes from a very wealthy family, he's had the best in education, travelled the world, and all the privileges money can buy.

Ricky comes from a poor background, his father died when he was a child and his mother has had to struggle to raise him and his four brothers and sisters. He left school at 15 and worked at a lot of menial jobs before working his way up to the foreman's job he now has.

Both men work for a company that has just had the employees' pension plan embezzled. Which one is most likely to be the embezzler: John, who has everything money can buy and wants to live the high life without regard to the cost to anyone else? Or Ricky, who's never had a break until he got this job with the company, and now he wants to start his own business?

On the surface, you'd think Ricky would be the likely candidate to steal the cash.

John: everything has come easily, but he still feels the need to prove himself worthy of his overbearing and over-achieving father. The pension money is his for the taking – even if he has to cook the books to do so. He may have gambling debts that are threatening him, but he doesn't need a stronger motive than competitiveness with his father – and he has the opportunity. Sometimes people in this position will do things just to prove they can, because they think they are smarter than everyone else and can get away with it. And even rich folk can get in over their heads…

Ricky – motivation to take money may be there if you give him a sick wife or some pressing debts. Problem is, he's doing better than he's ever done in his life – and he's been raised to work hard for everything he has. Why would he mess things up now? But is that the old 'poor but honest' cliché? Let's look at whether he would have an opportunity. Would he actually be able to cook the books even if he had the chance? Well, he works a lot of overtime and he has the keys to the offices. What if he's been taking accountancy classes because he wants to better himself still further? What if he's been taking computer classes for the same reason, and has a natural flair for hacking into other computer systems – like maybe the company's accounting system?

When you change your character's motivation, you may change your entire storyline. Interesting, eh?

EXERCISING THAT DREADED SAGGING MIDDLE

You've started your novel or short story and you've organized a brilliant opening to hook your reader's imagination and keep them turning the pages. Filled with excitement, you ride the wave of this wonderful new idea all the way – to chapter three.

Then, WHAM! The wave recedes and you're left gasping on the shore. Your Muse has abandoned you. Your idea looks about as exciting as a damp squib. Already you're wondering why you ever thought anyone would ever be interested in this in the first place. Your characters are bullying you. They refuse to do as they are told – or maybe they disappear from your pages altogether, hiding like wallflowers and refusing to come out and play.

By this stage you're probably toying with the idea of buying a nice new paper shredder and wondering why you thought you could be a writer. Or maybe even why you ever thought you wanted to be one.

Welcome, my friends, to the Dreaded Sagging Middle.

But it doesn't have to be this way – you can tighten up that sagging middle and find your way to The End and Happily Ever.

The middle of the book is where most of the action takes place. Pacing here is a big help – don't fall into the trap of putting in every little detail, every move your characters make, and every scene change in glorious Technicolor. No wonder your Muse is yawning! Keep your writing tight, bright, and crisp. When you were filled with the excitement of that brilliant beginning, you knew your reader didn't need to know what the hero ate for breakfast, or how many cups of coffee your heroine drank while waiting for the villain to arrive and make her life exciting again.

If they didn't need those details at the beginning, why do they need them now? Chop out all extraneous descriptive pieces, surgically remove all actions that don't take your story any further, and you'll see your sagging middle begin to perk up there and then.

The secret is that all detail, all descriptive prose, all actions, must be an essential part of the story. It's only essential to the story that the hero missed his bus if missing the bus is the device by which he is introduced to another story character, is vulnerable to attack by villains, or loses his job and is forced to take measures that permit the action and plot to move forward.

If the paragraph about the missed bus doesn't show us anything about his character, if it doesn't introduce a further character or piece of action, if it doesn't move the story forward, out it goes. Remember, most publishers have a limit to the size of book they will publish. Save that precious space for the essentials of your story instead of filling it up with extraneous detail.

A good way to keep the story moving is to have your chapters roughly plotted – even if it's just a short sentence on an index card. *Polly Meets Mac and Agrees to Visit Granddad With Him* may well be enough to jog your memory about the action that's needed for the chapter you're writing.

But no one is going to clamour to read the details of that sentence. What you need is to have a hook at the beginning of each chapter, and a hook at the end. So, when you start writing this chapter, you're going to have an exciting statement or action to draw the reader in. How does Sally Meet Mac? Is it prearranged? Is she late? Does she even know who Mac is?

A good opening hook for this chapter could be something like: *Sally paused at the door. Maybe she should just call the whole thing off – it wasn't too late to turn around and leave……..*

But we know she's going to go with Mac to see Granddad. Granddad is going to import a piece of information that will move the story along. They may have an adventure on the way to Granddad's House – maybe being run off the road by the Big Bad Wolf, perhaps? – but once there, everything seems to quiet down. Until Granddad says: "I needed to see you because your Grandmother has been kidnapped."

Okay, that's your closing hook – or something like it. It doesn't have to be a statement. Granddad could clutch a photo of Grannie and burst into tears. Or he could keel over with a heart attack from the stress. But it closes your chapter with a BOOM and your reader is going to want to turn the page to the next chapter just to see how it all works out.

Avoid putting in scenes just for the sake of it. Remember your plot, remember what you want your characters to do, and stick with it. If you find your characters are going off at tangents, that's a good time to stop and listen to them. Or at least, consider what it is that's going on that differs so much from your plot. Could it be that your plot isn't working and your subconscious is trying to tell you *'It's better this way'* ? Or is it that you're afraid to write the actions that do move the plot along?

Perhaps you've not done the research you need, so you're avoiding that shaky ground because you are not really sure what you're talking about. The answer to that is simple, of course – Get Thee Out and Research.

Maybe it's a sex scene – lots of people have trouble with these because they imagine their loved ones reading over their shoulders and it's, well, just plain embarrassing.

Get over it. If the scene is important to the plot, if it brings your characters' relationship to a new level, if it opens the way for further conflict or betrayal, then get the scene written.

Some writers are so determined to get that sex scene in that they force themselves to go into clinical detail. Yuck! You don't need this. If you can't write a graphically erotic scene naturally – and lots of writers can't – then remember that 'less is more' and keep the details sensually misty.

Don't put in action just for the sake of it, any more than you'd put in descriptive prose for the sake of it. Action should be consistent with the characters' behaviour and their motivation, and consistent with the plot and environment. Stuff that isn't, sticks out like a sore thumb, stops your reader dead in her tracks and contributes to the sag of your middle.

Once you've swirled through the excitement of beginning the book and setting the scene for your story, the Middle is the place to start introducing secondary characters, bring in sub plots and show the obstacles that your characters have to overcome.

Secondary characters add to the realism of your story – after all, no-one lives in a vacuum – but they can also be used to add information that couldn't be easily worked in otherwise, and as support characters to help out the main characters.

Sub plots are essential to most stories. They add texture, richness, and add extra excitement. Nobody has only one thing happening in their lives at once, so don't turn your story into a one-horse race.

In the middle is the place to sprinkle your clues, the hints and morsels of information that like a trail of breadcrumbs lead your reader to The End. Make sure your ending doesn't occur without every aspect of the dénouement being foreshadowed by hints and clues dropped throughout the middle of the book. A red herring or two, a false signpost, will all add to the excitement.

Your hero will have to identify and climb over obstacles in his path as he traverses the middle of his story. Make the going hard but not impossible, and allow your reader to travel with him by having access to all these little clues. Of course, knowing the clues doesn't mean he won't be surprised by your dramatic ending!

By now you should have been so busy reading this, plotting your chapters, adding clues, hints, obstacles, secondary characters and texture – all within the scope of the story and your main characters' motivations – that you've rolled right past the middle. Looking back, you will see that the middle is taut and exciting, with not a sag in sight!

Soon you will be typing in The End. What a wonderful feeling! But finishing your novel isn't really the end – in the next chapter we look at editing and sending your work out to a publisher.

No Frills Writing - Lesson 9 Assignments

Writing Exercise 9:1: Take a long look at your main characters, with the help of the character sheets you drew up. What is their motivation for their actions in the story? Can you see layers of motivation, the Why? based on who these people are and their past experience and background as you planned it on your character sheets?

Writing Exercise 9:2: Write the next chapter of your rough first draft!

CHAPTER TEN

In this chapter we're going to talk about editing your work, formatting your novel and submitting your work to publishers and agents.

The End is in sight. Here are a few tips to keep you working without getting side-tracked:

1) **Test** the strength of your idea by writing a 'logline' – a couple of sentences that capture the essence of your planned book.

2) **Consider** your schedule – decide how much time you can spend, and pencil that into your calendar.

3) **Focus**. Okay, you've a gazillion ideas running around in your head, but you can actually only write one book at a time. Choose your plot, roll up your sleeves and get to it'

4) **While working on your novel,** you'll no doubt be inundated with lots of other book ideas, some feasible, some not. And you'll be tempted to test them, to write a few pages, to start an outline…..don't!

5) **Instead, keep a record of your ideas.** Write a logline, jot down any odd paragraphs or outline ideas that come to mind. Then be ruthless: open your Ideas file (or start one if you haven't already) and save that wonderful new idea to it. You can always add other bits and pieces that come to you and belong to that idea. But don't give in to the temptation to start writing a whole new book – not until you've finished your wip. That's Work In Progress.

6) **Don't** allow yourself to get side-tracked and wind up with a 100,000 page novel that really is an amalgam of all the novel ideas that came to you while writing this one. Put the ideas in the ideas file, and concentrate on writing this book.

7) **Lots of famous authors** write in several genres, but the catch word here is famous. If you're just setting out, choose your genre and perfect your style, complete and polish a novel. Then you can start something new while you're pitching the finished work to a publisher.

EDITING YOUR WORK

. You've finished your first draft. Now it's time to read through your work thoroughly. Read with a reader's eye first of all, then with an editor's – imagine your sixth grade English teacher. The first run through you are looking for major problems: plot lines that don't work, people who need fleshing out, dialogue that's flat, sentences and phrases that are awkward.

And you'll need to keep a sharp lookout for inaccuracies, too – double check on any foreign words, technical words, colloquialisms, etc., to be sure you are using them correctly. Check for realism – if your character is a surgeon, is it likely that he'd work in the garden without gloves to protect his hands?

And character realism – if a character is a recovering alcoholic, would she really arrange to meet her friends in a bar? Well, maybe she would – but give it a context of why? This is also the time to be honest with yourself – does your plot line really carry the story? Is it strong enough?

Keep a notebook by your computer while you read through your MS – or on your desk alongside your hardcopy if you've printed it out. Write the page number and a note about anything that causes you concern, or jars you out of the story.

Running spelling and grammar checks will often throw up some problems you hadn't thought about before – such as clumsy or passive sentences where an active sentence would enliven your prose. Beware spelling suggestions, though – the computer's spell check may insist on putting in 'which' where you want that, or 'there' where it should be 'their', and any number of other spelling and grammar errors.

Watch for the use of names – make sure each character ends the book with the same name he/she started out with! But over and above that, don't use the name too often. If there are only two people in a scene, you don't need to constantly use either name. It should be obvious who is speaking or acting from the context. The same applies to 'tags' – dialogue markers such as 'he said' or 'she said'.

Don't be dismayed if this process shows a lot of points that need correction. Many of these will be simple typos, and most will be points which need clarification rather than a total rewrite. This is good – it means your next draft will be more polished, and more polished is more publishable. And it's much, much better that you catch those really dumb errors than have to bear the embarrassment of sending your work to an editor and having her find them.

So, now you've completed work on the next draft. How do you feel about it? Is it ready to be sent out? You're sure? You're just itching to get it into an envelope and out the door? STOP Right There!

Put your work in a folder and put it away, preferably in a dark place where you won't be tempted to peek. For short work and articles, a day's respite might do. For bigger work and especially novels, a couple of weeks or more of stewing time is required. Then you're going to go back and read your work with new eyes.

After a break, it's almost as if you're reading someone else's work, which is good, because it allows you to be ruthless without hurting the feelings of someone really important – you!

Now, working on a new hard copy of your work, you're going to read it as if it were the first time you'd come across it. Read it as a reader. If anything jars with you, pushes you out of the story, or is an obvious mistake, then write a note in the margin, and maybe a corresponding longer note in your trusty notebook (don't forget to cite the page number, though).

Many writers read their work aloud. It might make you feel silly, but it really is a good exercise, especially with passages that you may be finding difficult. Do this preferably when there is no-one else present unless you're tough-skinned and can take the criticism of your nearest and dearest, who by the time you've droned your way to page 245, may not be very sympathetic.

So, how does it sound? Does it flow? Did you feel silly speaking the lines you've given your characters in dialogue? If so, how do you think they feel? And how do you think your readers will feel about the characters with dumb or awkward speech patterns that they can't believe in? Again, make notes.

We're not correcting right now, just thinking and observing and mulling things over. Nothing shows up awkward or clumsy sentence structure like reading out loud.

Take a break when you've finished.

Back to work.

Now's the time for some serious thinking. Read the notes you've made. Do you still agree with them on a second reading? Have you checked the possibly wrongly-used or wrongly-spelled words? Made sure your characters actions, speech patterns and clothing, etc., are consistent?

So, back to the computer. Make the changes on your digital copy. It may seem a huge job, but you'll be able to get through it quickly after so much thought and consideration.

A word of warning here – don't fall into the trap of adding extra plot lines. It can happen a lot during editing, but really only confuses the issue and you may wind up with several books in one. Only add things that will strengthen your existing plot lines. Make your work better by solving the problems you've found – don't try to validate them by adding new plot lines.

This is also a good spot to consider your word count.

If the editor asked for a 2,000-word article or the publisher wants a 70,000 word novel; you'll be dead in the water if you send a thousand words or ten thousand words over that limit. And don't think that because it's truly beautiful prose, they'll make an exception. They won't. Stephen King refers to the process of 'killing your darlings' and it's a good way to put it. But the result is that you've got good, tight writing – and if it works for King, who are we to argue?

Now you've got the changes done. Your characters are behaving properly. Dressing and talking authentically, and there are no huge gaps in the action that leave your reader wondering *what happened?* Or worse, leave your reader asleep.

Run the spelling and grammar check tool again. Pay attention to what it says. Do be very aware that the spellchecker may not distinguish between certain words: i.e.; there, their; red, read; die, dye. Also, the spellchecker will not be able to tell you if you've used the wrong word – it couldn't care less if you put cheek instead of check; blast instead of baste.

These may be typos that could give your sentence a whole new meaning, but spellchecker doesn't mind so long as they are spelled correctly. It's up to you to be vigilant. You don't want any of your characters blasting the Christmas turkey or slapping their cheek down on the counter – except in certain special circumstances, of course!

And now you are going to read through it all again. Maybe you feel like you know it off by heart, maybe you need to set it aside again for a while. But this is important stuff, so trudge along with me. Keep a sharp eye out for inconsistencies – make sure you keep all the peripheral descriptive details correct. Your reader will note if a character has blue eyes in chapter three and they've turned brown by chapter six; or if she's living in a ground floor condo in chapter one but having to take the elevator up to her home in chapter five.

It may sound like a no-brainer, too, but again check the names are right all through the book. Don't scoff – you'd be surprised how easy it is to make these little errors that throw your reader right out of the story.

FORMATTING

Once everything is right, it's time to ensure your formatting is correct. Type your name and contact information on the top left hand corner of your title page, then the title centred and about halfway down the page, with your own name underneath it – pseudonyms come later!

Normally, chapters start about seven double spaced lines down the page – and always on a new page. I usually put the chapter in bold capitals, like this: **CHAPTER ONE.** No need to underline. Skip a line and start your work. A popular guideline is 25 lines to a page, around ten words to a line. This is supposed to give 250 words per page. How do you know you've approximately ten words to a line, without counting over 300 pages of copy? Count the words of five lines, divide by five. If the result is nine or eleven, or thereabouts, you're okay.

If you are applying this format to a document you've already written, go to Edit, press Select All so that all your work is selected, then follow the instructions.

In the paragraph box, click on **Indents and Spacing**. If you are starting out fresh you can miss these steps and go straight to the Format drop down menu and on to **Indents & Spacing.**

Click on Paragraph. A box opens and you add the following information:
>Alignment: Left
>Indentation
>Left: 0" or 0.1" or 0.2" (Should give you a 1 inch margin.)
>Right: 0"
>Spacing: Before: 0 pt
>After: 0 pt
>Outline Level: Body Text
>Line Spacing: Exactly At: 25 pt

>Now click on **Line and Page Breaks**. Make sure the box next to each thing is left unchecked, including **Widow/Orphan Control**. Click **OK**.

Don't worry if all this formatting seems like too much computer-ese. If you're using MSWord in the Office 2010 format, you'll find a manuscript template under the new document key that will allow you to type your wip directly into the template in an acceptable style. As writers we need to use all the tools at our fingertips to make the packaging of our work as simple as possible.

This formatting applies to just about anything you are going to send out, from articles to non-fiction books and novels.

Email Submissions:

If you are sending your work as an email attachment – and many agents and publishers now accept submissions only by email – you still need to format your manuscript like this, in double spacing. It makes it both easier to read for the editor and easier for her to put notes in if she wishes. Check the submission guidelines to see if there are other requirements.

The first page for articles would be different – you would not use a cover page and title, but go straight into the article about halfway down the page.

If you are sending out a book, check the publishers' requirements. Most want a query letter and a synopsis. Some want the first three chapters as well.

The synopsis should be fairly easy because you did a pretty comprehensive outline for your work. So you flesh out the outline, usually using present tense and keeping it terse. This should be less than seven pages, and some publishers want even shorter synopses. It should be short and succinct, but get your writing style, voice, and the highlights of your story across. And don't be coy and secretive about your ending. The editor isn't going to steal it, but she won't like to be left on a cliff-hanger, either – that sort of thing is for the back cover blurb. The editor needs to know how your story ends.

And I cannot stress enough how clean your work must be. Use a clear 12 point type – Times New Roman is popular, as is Arial or Dark Courier. If sending out a hard copy, use white paper. It doesn't have to be heavy, expensive bond, 20 pound bond is generally the best choice.

No cute gimmicks, like cartoon characters or coloured inks. You may be submitting a romance, but pretty pink paper with a roses and hearts pattern will not win you brownie points with an editor or agent.

We've already talked about query letters, so all you need now is to put it all together. Check with the publisher or agent's website, blog or listing in Writer's Market, Writers' and Artists' Yearbook, Writers' Digest, or whichever source you are using for the submission requirements.

Meticulously follow the publishers' or agents' submission guidelines. This can't be stressed enough.

FORMATTING FOR ELECTRONIC SUBMISSIONS

No discussion about formatting would be complete in the current market, especially when many publishers, including traditional print publishers, are asking for submissions to be formatted for digital, or electronic, publishing. There are many reasons for this, including the fact that most submissions are done by email and in all too many cases the formatting may not be recognised by the program receiving it, and you have a lot of extraneous symbols, etc., suddenly appearing in your email text and your (once) beautifully formatted manuscript..

Here's a general guideline for formatting for electronic submissions, but it's wise to remember that publishers often have their own requirements listed on their websites. Some require a short query letter and, if they're interested in seeing more, will send you a list of their formatting requirements. You can save time by having as much as the formatting done in readiness!

The first thing to check is what kind of document the company accepts - usually it's .doc or .rtf, although some will request a .pdf. As we said earlier, always make sure you are sending exactly what they ask for! Often with email submissions, the publisher or agent requires a short query letter with all the usual details (see section on query letters) along with two or three paragraphs describing your plot, in the case of fiction, or your subject angle, in the case of non-fiction.

You'll be asked to include a sample of the book, anything from the first two pages right up to the first three chapters. Most publishers seem to require this in the body of the email because they are reluctant to open attachments because of the risk of viruses. They usually stress in their submissions guidelines that they will not open attachments and queries with attachments will not be read. See why it is so important to read guidelines carefully?

Some much used formatting tricks turn into odd symbols or simply don't translate well at the re3civer's end. For example, don't use your tab key to make paragraphs. Most word processing programs now have an automatic default that sets your paragraph indents when you hit the Enter key and begin a new paragraph - usually at .5 inch.

How do you know if you're using tabs? Click Edit, Find, then click on Special Characters, and again on Tab, then Find Next. If a marker like a right handed arrow in brackets appears, then you have tabs. Go through your manuscript and remove all these markers, then reformat using the finds and replace box. All the paragraphs that were tabbed will no longer be indented.

Next, you right click on each paragraph, click paragraph on the drop down menu that appears, and in the Special box, click First Line. This properly indents each paragraph.

You may notice that some of your centred headings, etc., are too far over to one side. This is because you have tabbed the paragraph that the line starts with. Remove the tab, as above, and then click on centre - the words should be exactly in the centre now. Chapter headings are usually in bold and centred.

You will almost certainly be using the header space - this is where you put the title of your book and your name. It's also where page numbers go but again, check the submission guidelines as many publishers, especially e-publishers, do not want page numbers in the manuscript. Don't use tabs or the spacebar in headers or footers.

Scene breaks usually consist of **** OR *****.

Use the page break function at the end of each chapter, otherwise your next chapter won't start on a new page.

Use the File-Options-Proofing-Autocorrect-Autoformat facility and click on the box for converting hyphens to em dashes. Do not use -- as an em dash.

In print it's tempting to use three or more periods as an ellipsis (when you want to show a thought or sentence trailing off...) In your e-submission, you should use three periods with spaces before, between, and after each one: . . .

Put on space after a period at the end of sentences, unless the guidelines ask for two.

Check the guidelines about quotation marks - some publishers want smart quotes, others want curly quotes. Use you find and replace action if you discover you need to change them.

Don't use any unusual fonts - Times New Roman or Courier are the most requested.

Once upon a time in print publishing, if you wanted something to be in italics, you always left it in regular type and underlined it. Printing techniques have changed and now if you want something in italics, *you simply type it into your manuscript in italics.*

This may all seem like a lot of fuss, especially if you have to go over an entire manuscript and make changes, but proper formatting can make the difference between your work being read by the publisher or not.

FINDING A PUBLISHER OR AGENT

This is where you will need to take out the notes you made way back in Chapter One – remember those book store visits where you checked out the sort of books you wanted to write, and the publishers who 'pubbed' them?

Now we're going to take a look at the publishers a little more closely, and look for other companies who may be a good fit for the work you've just finished. A copy of Writers' & Artists' Yearbook, or Writer's Market, depending on whether you're in Europe or North America, will be useful. However, the choice is more to do with your location and personal preference, as both contain information about publishers internationally.

There is also a humongous amount of information on publishers on the Internet, available for free. I just did a quick search for *Publishers of Mystery Novels* on Google, and came up with 27,000,000 results in 19 seconds. Phew! That's pretty daunting, yes? Not all the results were for publishers – Google pulled up some interesting sites for articles on publishing and articles on writing, too, which were included in the search results. And some of the results were a bit iffy – companies that wanted to be paid to publish your work, for example.

They're known as **Vanity Publishers,** and as a general rule, if a company asks for money to publish your work, you should turn around and run. Fast.

There are exceptions to that. One is that you really want to be published and are willing to tout your book around to flush out as many sales as you can. Or you just want a few copies to show off to friends and relatives. Watch out for poor quality printing and binding, and editing/proofreading. Also, make sure the quote you get is for all the services you're looking for – sometimes there are unexpected extras put on your bill as the process is underway.

Caveat Emptor, right? Buyer Beware.

Then there are some good Print On Demand 'publishers' around, such as Amazon and CreateSpace, Lightning Source, Lulu.com and Smashwords, to name a few. They all have different criteria for publishing, and different services, etc., but a lot of writers who choose to go the Indie, or Independent publishing route, find these POD companies can be just the ticket. Again, read through their pitches carefully, and don't sign on the dotted line until you know what you're getting into.

There's quite a trend nowadays for 'Indie' or independent publishing, where a writer publishes her own work. It's an exciting field, where you get to make all the decisions for your book and in the process acquire new skills, such as book formatting. That's how this book came to be in your hands, and I've had fun with it so far!

You also have the choice as to whether you go ebook or print or both, and when – as well as setting the price that suits you.

Looking at ebooks in particular, the decision is whether to set a low price and go for lots of sales, or whether to set a higher price and see what happens.

If you go this route there are a number of things to watch for. You may decide to buy a publishing package with one of the companies named above, who will do the formatting (book layout) for you as this can be difficult. They'll also help with cover art, printing, etc. and there are some really good deals out there.

Or you may decide to do everything yourself – it's a steep learning curve but well worth the experience, especially if you are considering doing more than one book. Use the Internet – there are lots and lots of articles and blogs out there on various aspects of publishing your own work.

Now, assuming you're not going the Indie route, we come to the agent /publisher question. It's really up to you whether you go after an agent or a publisher first.

A good agent can be a real career maker, helping the writer to hone her craft, find a publisher, sort out contract details, negotiate advances, and make career plans.

A good publisher can put your book in the spotlight; get it into the hands of distributors and bookstores, as well as giving you the comforting knowledge that you'll get royalties on a regular basis if you have sales. If you get an advance, you'll have to pay that back from royalties in most cases – but if your sales don't meet the required amount of money to pay back your advance, don't panic. They won't make you pay back the advance, but do check this out in your contract.

Always, always, read your contract carefully!

However, a lot of agents won't look at a new writer without some publishing credits under his/her belt. And most of the big publishers won't look at an unagented writer who hasn't already got a proven publishing and sales record.

Which is a kind of Catch 22, isn't it?

If you are considering submitting to a particular publisher or agent, take a look at Preditors & Editors (do a Google search) and check if there are any complaints against them. If you see 'recommended' you'll know that other writers have been impressed with that particular agent or publisher. If you see complaints or not recommended, then again, Caveat Emptor.

Check the bookstore shelves to see what the publisher you have in mind is doing. Look at the 'acknowledgement' or 'thanks' page to see if the author of books you like mentions their agent. Ask around on authors' lists online, or at your writers' group. Find out who your fellow writers recommend, and who they suggest you stay away from.

But in the final analysis, it all comes down to you. You must be in control of your writing future, as you would be with any other job or venture that's important to you.

WRAP-UP: HOW TO SUBMIT YOUR MATERIAL:

Always check with the publisher you intend to target as to what they want in a submission package. The information is usually on their web page. Be aware that some publishers will not look at anything directly from the writer – they will only deal with agents.

In that case, you need to put together a submission package for the agent – and you'd employ the same kind of research in finding an agent as you would a publisher. They're listed in droves on web sites and you can often send a brief query letter or email to ask if they're willing to look at your work.

Some publishers and agents ask for a query letter to start with. Others ask for a query, synopsis, and the first three chapters. Some want you to send the whole manuscript. Don't think that if you send the full manuscript even if they don't ask for it – or even the first three chapters - that they'll read it and be captivated by your prose. Many will simply send it back or bin it, if they haven't asked to see it. The trick with publishers, all the way down the line, is to give them what they ask for!

This is what should go into that package (depending on what the publisher requests):

1) A brief cover letter, or query letter, stating who you are, the title of your manuscript and (very briefly) what it is about. I like to start the query letter with my logline/blurb for the story. Here's the one for Resort to Murder:

Dear (editor's Name)

Re: My Romantic Suspense Novel, Resort to Murder

Falsely disgraced police detective Ellie Fitzpatrick is prepared to face a vicious killer to redeem herself but is she also brave enough to make peace with the man she loves? When her meteoric career crashed and burned after she was accused of accepting bribes from thugs running a protection racket, Ellie is suspended from the job she loves and believes herself abandoned not only by police colleagues but by her lover, Detective Liam Reilly. She is called back to work when a biography of a serial killer she arrested suggests the man may be innocent. Reilly vows to protect Ellie from the gang who tried to frame her and the vicious killer who's stalking her. Can she trust him with her life?

2) Then say why you are the person to write this book. This includes any relevant experience you may have, such as a degree in psychology or a certificate in forensic science.

3) You will also make sure your contact information is stated very plainly in the letterhead, with the book title and your name on all other pieces of paper you include. It has happened that an editor has been interested in a submission but hasn't been able to contact the author because there was no contact info – imagine how frustrating that would be!

4) You should also add a brief Author Bio – this is written in third person, and states your writing experience, published credits, etc.

5) A short – no more than two or three pages unless the publishers' guidelines state otherwise - synopsis of your book. This is always written in the present tense and can begin with the same hook you use to start your story. Then list in a very readable way who your characters are, the events of the story, what motivates them, how they benefit and change and grow through the events of the story. Basically, how your characters get what they want. Keep it brief, and don't try being coy by ending on a cliff-hanger – the editor wants and needs to know how your story ends, but isn't going to buy your manuscript just so you'll let him/her into the secret. He/she is more likely to be irritated by this ploy and return your work. ***This is your opportunity to display your writing voice and style, so spend some time on it!***

6) If requested, send the first three chapters of your book. These will be neatly and cleanly typed, free of typos, and you'll have checked and double checked to be sure that spelling and grammar are correct, that all factual references are in order, and that the whole thing is as smooth and polished as you can make it – and that it meshes with the synopsis! Your cover page will have your name, address, phone/fax/and email contact info on the top left hand side, no page number, and on the right hand top corner you'll have 'estimated' word count. Your title will be centred halfway down the page with your name underneath. On succeeding pages, you'll have your name and the book title on the left hand side, and page number on the top right hand corner.

7) Most submissions are done by email these days, and you should carefully check the publisher's requirements. Most ask just for the query letter first, and may ask for the first three chapters and synopsis. Most also insist that they won't open attachments - given the danger of getting an email virus, this is understandable. Everything will go in the body of the email, unless you are at the stage where they want to see the entire manuscript – at which point they probably trust you enough to send this large file as an attachment.

ALWAYS KEEP A COPY OF YOUR MANUSCRIPT AND SYNOPSIS.
Never, ever send a publisher your only copy – things do get lost, you know.

If sending a hard copy by snail mail, buy a padded envelope big enough to accommodate the whole package comfortably. You'll need a letter-sized thin sheet of cardboard. Place your manuscript on this, and put an elastic band around both ms. and cardboard. On top of this goes the synopsis, then the author bio if you're including one, then the cover letter on the very top.

The whole thing is then held together by another elastic band. NO STAPLES! You can, if necessary, use a paperclip to hold your letter together. Now, on the bottom of all this you'll need an envelope for the return of your work – self-addressed and stamped with the same amount of postage it costs you to send the package.

More and more publishers – especially those in the U.S.A. are refusing to return manuscripts and will ask only for a stamped self-addressed business sized envelope for them to send you a letter of rejection or acceptance. It's also useful to include a stamped, self-addressed postcard with the name of your manuscript and 'received' written on it. That's for them to send back to let you know they've received your package. If you don't do that you'll never know all your hard work has gone astray in the mail until you've wasted several months or more waiting to hear back from the publisher or agent.

International Reply Coupons (IRCs) were traditionally used for return postage to other countries, but these are being phased out and many publishers don't want them. So, if you're sending work abroad, you'll have to get stamps from that country. You can send an international bankers' draft in the amount for postage, but that's expensive and most publishers don't like them because of bank fees. Go online to the postal service site of the receiving country and order stamps. Or get a friend in that country to send you stamps – whatever way you can work it!

Again, always send what the publisher is asking for – usually a query letter to start with, or query/synopsis/ first three chapters or a combination of these. If they write back and ask for the entire manuscript, be sure to write 'requested material' on the envelope when you send the full manuscript, so that your work goes straight to the requesting editor instead of ending up on the slush pile.

REJECTION LETTERS – STEPPING STONES TO SUCCESS?

It's very rare for a writer to get a contract on their first novel on its very first query. I'm sure it must happen occasionally, but for the majority of us, it's a question of try, try, and try again.

Once you start sending your work out into the world, you are going to meet with the inevitable rejection. It may be very hard not to take it personally – after all that work, to receive a rejection can be devastating. It always sounds as though your work isn't good enough, even though there are many reasons that work is rejected.

These include submitting your MS to a publisher who doesn't publish that genre; or that the publisher has already signed a very similar story. It may be that they don't feel your story is right for them for a number of reasons, or simply that your story didn't appeal to the person who read it.

After all, reading taste is very subjective – I'm sure that you, like me, have read bestselling books that you simply couldn't get into. You may have purchased books that have won prestigious prizes and found that you simply didn't like the plot or the characters or perhaps the writing style.

Like I said, it's all subjective. Grow a thick skin and decide to embrace your rejections as the stepping stones towards your writing success.

Yes, I said embrace your rejections.

When you first start out your rejections may come as form letters, perhaps even without a proper signature.

Later, you'll get signed letters addressed to you personally from an editor or agent. Painful as it may be, at least they're taking you seriously. Some of these people may suggest that, while the enclosed MS Isn't what they're looking for, they would like to see any further work you produce. Eureka!

Later still, you'll receive letters with notes explaining why your work was rejected. Better yet, the editor or agent may take the time – and these are busy people – to make a few comments as to how the work could be improved, or what they particularly didn't like about it.

Sometimes they even suggest you correct the problems and resubmit. Do it quickly and cleanly, addressing your work directly to the person who signed the letter.

One caveat here: These recommendations as a general rule will improve your story. However, it may be that the editor or agent wants you to change a story line, a character, or a scene to an extent that you can hardly recognise your work or that the theme is compromised.

They may believe that this will make your work more saleable but in the final analysis, it's up to you how much you wish to change. If you feel your work is being devalued or compromised in theme or ethics, then it's time to dig in your heels and send it out to another editor.

Stephen King received enough rejection letters to paper the walls of a small bedroom, and was told that his work was not commercial. Ditto for J.K. Rowling, creator of the Harry Potter books, who was told that modern children weren't interested in magic and wizards. They are just two of the many bestselling authors who refused to give in to rejection depression and believed strongly enough in their work to keep on plugging away until they achieved publication.

Like I said, it's all subjective.

Treat your rejection letters as stepping stones to your publishing success. Learn from them. Consider carefully the comments you receive and whether you feel they improve your work, but don't take it all personally.

Above all, don't let a rejection destroy your dream. Keep on writing and submitting, keep on honing your writing craft, and someday you'll see your name on the cover of a brand new book.

Now you've edited and polished your MS until it glows. It's time to get out your list of publishers and agents and submit your work for publication.

Congratulations – you've reached the finish line!
Bask in the glory for a few minutes. Then it's time to start a whole new book!

ABOUT THE AUTHOR

Glenys O'Connell is the published author of mystery and romantic suspense novels, children's books, non-fiction books and award winning plays. This book grew from the creative writing course of that same name that she has been teaching online and in the classroom for nine years. She began her writing career as a journalist in the UK, Ireland & Canada, and now lives and works in Ontario, Canada with her husband, four grown up children and two spoiled cats. She can be contacted at RomanceCanBeMurder@hotmail.ca or through her web page at www.glenysoconnell.com

Made in the USA
Lexington, KY
26 August 2012